Endorsements

The book is as vibrant and innovative as the author himself. I am sure it will be a handy guide to people of all ages from different walks of life, to help them to understand the complicated web of life and sail through turbulent times with ease. I wish him all the very best and expect him to give us many more books in future.. "

Sonali Sinha
Sr. Director and Principal
Rayat Bahra Group, Chandigarh / Shimla

I picked up the book, wanted to critically examine how an Indian writer can do justice with such topics, I could not sleep and found it to be a story book, full of entertainment and full of learnings. Surely going to be Best Seller in shortest possible time.

R. K. Bhandari
Director
Banarsidas Chandiwala Institute of Hotel Management and Catering Technology

As a journalist who write on travel and hospitality, I had numerous opportunities to interact with Mr Behl, as well as listen to his lectures on human resource development in the past. He is professional to the core with in-depth knowledge on the subject and an excellent motivational speaker. I'm sure that his literary venture -Winning is Everything will benefit a whole new generation of readers. I wish him all success.

P Krishna Kumar
Head -Delhi Bureau
Saffron Media -Travel Biz Monitor / Hospitality Biz

Having known Mr Deepak Behl for some years now, I have no hesitation in stating that his book-Winning is Everything would have pearls of wisdom for all and in particular the HR fraternity. Good luck and Godspeed!

Brig. Prakash Ghogale VSM
Director of Human Resources
Hyatt Regency Delhi

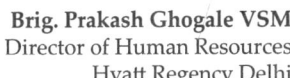

Deepak thinks differently, he is energetic, extremely sincere and helpful. I always knew that he has great thoughts and ideas and he would come up with this amazing book. He is respected and loved by the HR Heads of all hotels in the city. His team members love him and learn from him every time. Good Luck.

Neesha Mohapatra
Director of Human Resources
The Grand New Delhi

I have not known anybody who has written such a self-help book with full of stories, which are not only interesting but teach long lasting lessons resulting in a very positive overwhelming response, this will surely be a Best Seller.

Salman Azam Qureshi
Regional Director -Human Resources
Apeejay Surrendra Park Hotels

Congratulations for this long awaited book which is not merely a book but a complete philosophy. Great job done Deepak...Wish your book a great success in days to come.

Parag Bhatnagar
Director-Human Resources
The Suryaa New Delhi

Winning is Everything is an exceptional book, I would love to be with Deepak understanding some mantras to be a winner in life, otherwise also it is always a please to enjoy his power packed and motivational sessions.

Manish Sadhu
Director of Human Resources
SHERATON BANGALORE

Deepak has always been my motivational force. This book for sure will proof a prized possession for every individual. The title "Winning is Everything" in itself is a road to success.

Shikha Bhadauria
Assistant Manager Marketing
Choice Hotels India

I have always found Deepak to be a hardworking, committed, dedicated and pleasant to work with. He has been very diligent and persevering in writing this book. "Winning is Everything" is a Masterpiece. Deepak has beautifully explained in simple words the intricacies of management principles. I am sure that the readers would be able to imbibe the message conveyed.

Vinay Kumar Singh
General Manager-Personnel
Old World Hospitality Pvt Ltd At India Habitat Centre

It is infectious....You start reading it and you would not leave it till the time it gets finished. Winning is Everything is all about you, you as an individual, you as a professional, you as a person. It explains how to succeed, what to do and how to be on the path of winning. It is a convincing book as it is written with loads of examples (linking to your life) and it is easy to understand something in life with examples. This is going to be one of the hot selling books pretty soon.

Amit Caroli
HR and Quality Manager
InterContinental Eros

This book captures amazing management mantras of Deepak, whom I have always praised highly as a trainer, good luck Deepak, great going, you have written your success story. I think this book will be a significant addition in my personal library.

Surendra Singh
Dy.General Manager (F&B) Integra,
Hospitality & Facility Management Ltd.

Writing this book was not Mr. Behl's decision, we pressurised him to do so, how can you not justify your name – 'Deepak', whose work is to enlighten the world. Thank you for this Masterpiece.

Wg. Cdr. S. L. Soni
Ex. – Chief Security Officer
The Oberoi, New Delhi

Deepak never takes shortcuts in life for anything, may it be writing. I am confident 'Winning is Everything' will set another milestone of records. My best wishes are always with Deepak.

Ashish Broota
Kitchen Stewarding Manager
Jaypee Vasant Continental, Jaypee Hotels

It is an inspiring interesting read which makes u think, "I always had it in me, why didn't I realise it" or "This was always around me, why didn't I see it". It is a book about recognising yourself and your surroundings. It clears up your vision and organises the clutter in your mind. It melts away all your procrastination and suddenly you don't want to waste even a second of your life without moving one step towards success. It picks up all the little things in our lives and shows us how those are the building blocks for our future. Simple examples and stories which make you understand how each small decision of today shapes your tomorrow and coming years.

Nivedita Awasthi
Executive Housekeeper
Hilton Hotels

Reading this book is an experience. The book captures winning as an attitude and how the same can be cultivated. This book shall leave you with one purpose in life that is how to emerge as a winner in test we call -life.

Monica Bose
Corporate Training Manager
Hilton Worldwide -India

It would not be wrong to say that this book is a Masterpiece for students, who would be entering in corporate sector. The selection of chapters in this book is abound in contents and very relevant with practical examples / experiences.

Anil Miglani
Dy. Human Resource Manager
Eros Hotel managed by Hilton

Deepak is a very passionate HR Professional, who carries a vast experience in various fields ranging from Police Services, MNC's and Hospitality Industry. With his diverse experience he has put together in his book, in a very simplistic manner, Management Mantras for young and budding talents of the future. The content of his book is not only for the youth, but also makes great reading and learning for Senior Managers in the Corporate World. I congratulate Deepak for bringing this dream of his to constructive reality

Vikas Sharma
General Manager
Starwood Hotels & Resorts Worldwide Inc

It gives me immense pleasure to endorse the book written by Mr. Deepak Behl, which covers the topics on Human Behaviour and tips on how to win over self. Mr. Behl has inculcated the human values to develop a youthful and a dedicated sprite amongst the Practitioners of Management through this book. I know Mr. Behl for the last 15 years as a student and as a teacher both. He is an excellent human being with a pleasant personality which is the basic force to bring out the potential from other human beings. I am confident this book shall be a source of inspiration and serve as a tool to develop capable human beings with a dynamic development in life. I wish Deepak a grand success"

Y K Sachdev
Director
DIMS Institute of Management Studies

Some books are to be tasted, others to be swallowed and some few to be chewed and digested. There is no doubt in my mind that Deepak Behl's book falls in this category, Superb…

Prof. Rituraj Kumar
Assistant Professor – HR
NIILM Centre for Management Studies

The book Winning is Everything authored by Mr. Deepak Behl is so elegantly written, explaining the winning mantras of life with the help of his rich & diverse life experiences. The 10 chapters of the book are like 10 steps of success ladder seems true & relevant for one and all who want to succeed in life. This book indeed is a masterpiece. I wish him all the best and anxiously look forward to this book becoming a best selling book of year 2012.

Prof. (Dr.) M. Sajnani
Director
Amity Institute of Travel & Tourism

I can say without battling an eyelid that just a simple handshake with Deepak is a motivating experience. His ideas are fresh and he has the exceptional ability to put them across in a very simple manner.

Rohit Manchanda
Dean -IIPM
Centre for Executive Communication
& Personality Development

I have met numerous professionals during my 24 years of corporate, consulting and academia and I found Deepak different than many. His passion, commitment to the situation and ability to communicate complex issues are his special qualities. He has touched quite sensitive aspects and doubts with students and have explained excellently, the young budding managers will stand to gain a lot from this book. It has been a sheer pleasure to have his association because he is our INTELLECT DELIGHT

Prof. S C Kapoor
Senior Professor – JIMS,
Executive Director, Third Millennium Business Resource Associates

Deepak Behl has written a remarkable book for those who want to succeed in life, so elegantly written and so understanding with the help of his stories and examples that it is going to be a gift for mankind.

Prof. S.C Bagri
Dean & Director
H.N.B Garhwal University
Founder President – Indian Hospitality Congress

Deepak's recipe of being successful in life is amalgamated with perfect blend of success, excellence and flawlessness -all so logically and skilfully tempered with the spices of real life experiences so as to develop ' Winners Recipe' of Success.
This is a must read book for budding management professionals and men of intellect.

Dr. Ashish Dahiya
Associate Professor – MD University Rohtak
Jt. Secretary – Indian Hospitality Congress

We are delighted and grateful to him as he has decided to share a piece of wisdom in the form of this book. The book is a composition of small stories to help everyone in understanding those facts of life which we generally ignore as those appear small things for everyone's self-big image. Surely this book will help executives to execute their plans towards achieving maximum results with minimum 'Smart Work'.

Parvinder Kumar
Director
Arise Business School, Delhi

You must have read and heard many success stories, after reading this book, you will have your own success story.

Gaurav Sharma
Administrative Officer
Ahlcon International School

I know Mr. Deepak Behl for last 12 years and witnessed his efforts to achieve excellence and perfection not only at professional front but in everything what ever he does. I am sure 'Winning is Everything' will be a great success because a true winner knows the secret of winning as Mr. Behl has shared his success mantras in this book. My best wishes are with him.

Atul Gaur
Director
Career Matrix Institute of Professional Studies

It was around 10 years ago during a session, that Mr. Deepak Behl ignited a spark in me to leave the comfort zone of a good, secure and steady job and to take a plunge in the harsh and challenging world of entrepreneurship. I am so glad that my GURU has finally penned down his experiences and GURU MANTRAs in this book, explained thoroughly via very simple and fascinating stories, which I am sure will guide and mentor a far larger audience than possible through direct lectures and help them in achieving their true potential.

Pushpinder Saluja
Director
Career Matrix Institute of Professional Studies

"Winning is Everything" is not simply a book; it is the way of life. Mr. Behl has broken the clutter of ideology and takes you to the journey of practical facets of life. Implementing the thoughts & guidelines of this book at every step of life would be the best compliment to the hard work of Mr. Behl. In the form of this book he has surely done the job of Bhagirath (An ancient Indian king) who took Ganga (The holy river of India) to the earth from heaven for the welfare of mankind. Being the Hindi translator of this book and a faculty in the field of management, I firmly believe that this book will prove itself a compulsory book for the students, professionals and everybody looking for success.

Dr. Arun Mittal
Assistant Professor – Birla Institute of Technology, Noida

Deepak is a master story teller and he weaves his magic in this book mixing sage advice with humour. He enlightens and he entertains. It is Panchatantra for the millennials. I could not put this book down. Some of these stories and lessons will stay with me for a long time.

Sandeep Kalra
Chief Executive, Integrated Power Utility, Canada

This new book by Deepak Behl provides a much-needed treatment of real and practical options for success aimed at professionals. It is comprehensive, highly readable, and replete with useful examples. Every management practitioner should have a copy of "Winning is Everything" on hand.

Sanjeev Dheer
CEO and Founder, Beyond West Consulting, Australia

Some books are written to be the best sellers in shortest possible time; this Indian Author has all the potential to be one, wishing this Indian Genius the best of luck.

Navin Sarin
Managing Director, Metropole Industries

This book inspires us to follow our own dreams and how to win a lost battle, knowing Deepak for so many years has been a wonderful experience, he has always had a positive outlook towards life and this book is a replica of what he is all about.

Anupam Luthra
Marketing / Content Manager, The Human Capital

This book captures unmatched management mantras of Deepak, whom I have always known and praised as a highly inspired trainer, a great leader, an excellent pear and an affectionate & kind human being. Good luck Deepak, great going; you have written your success story. I think this book will be a significant addition in my personal library.

Maj. Pratap Singh
VP and Head – Admin, Corporate Affairs and Facilities
Reliance Infrastructure Limited

Deepak's writing a book was never a surprise he has always worked with a lot of passion and enthusiasm in the field of HR, he has been a mentor and guide to a lot of people and has always been very helpful to colleagues and co-workers, his penning down a book is an extension to his nature of sharing and nurturing people around him .There are lots of self help books available in market what makes his apart from the rest is the hands on knowledge and experience he has gathered in his years of work. It is not theory but more practical, adaptable and implementable suggestions and techniques he has shared through his book which can actually help people pursue their dreams and work on the weak areas in life. I wish him all the best for the same.

Anjalee Ahuja
Managing Director
Cosmos Corporate Services Pvt Ltd

Deepak Behl is a Management Guru par excellence, his expertise in Leadership, Decision Making, Communication and Teamwork will help millions in succeeding in the corporate jungle where 'survival of the smartest' is the mantra.

Rekesh Seth
Senior Vice President -Group HR
Fedders Lloyd Corporation Ltd., Lloyd Group

A prodigious book that accelerates one's thrive for success and nevertheless elucidates those elementary, practical and feasible ways to achieve them in an extremely easy to understand language and stories from our lives. A must have package for everyone, be it a management student, corporate professional or for that matter a common man.

Puneet Kapoor
Senior Associate HR, NIIT Technologies

Not just another book on Mantra's of Success, a truly useful guide to what professionals can and should do comprehensive, focused and immediately useful. How to be successful is an articulate and highly readable synthesis of current thinking on success and a framework to apply this in real life situations. Integrates the research on Success and provides a what-to-do list of actions and useful examples. Importantly, this book differentiates itself in a field that has been over studied by driving the reader to the pure essence of Success Mantras and how each one of us, regardless of level or position, can become more personally proficient. If you read Deepak Behl's book and heed his practical advice, you will have a huge advantage the next time a problem arises and you will have the structure, policies and guidance to make the right decision. A must for aspiring managers who value their development and effectiveness

Vijay Dogra
Regional & Unit Head – IT
Hindalco Industries Limited, (Aditya Birla Group)

Deepak's vast knowledge, deep thoughts, management mantras & communication skills are par excellence. Well conceived ideas have yielded astonishing results in his book. Each Topic covered appears well balanced and at the right place. This book surely and shortly shall be among the best selling books; given the appealing simplicity with which it directly touches both heart and brain. A must read book for everyone aspiring to win in life and especially for those; sailing through rough weathers.

Y. P. Madan
Chairman cum MD
Point Blank Group of Companies

I know Deepak since my MBA days and he has always been not only a helping hand in management studies but a guiding source to all. I was really moved by the examples in the book which one can very well relate to in today's times. This book is surely going to steal the hearts of millions and would sell like hot cakes !

Sunil Buttan
Manager – Human Resources
PriceWaterhouseCoopers, Gurgaon, India

This book by Deepak Behl is undeniably one of the best books I have read in a long time. He brings forth all the variables that contribute to success for the reader, written in a format which is easiest to grasp. Wish that I had read this book 20 years ago, I would have gotten 'There' faster. Anyone who wants to be successful in life just needs this book and no more.

Deepak Mendiratta
Entrepreneur & Chief Driver, HII Group of Companies

I know Deepak from childhood, his zeal to succeed has taken him where he is today. He has written a remarkable book for those who want to be a winner in life. This book is written so gracefully that everyone can understand and adopt easily, and I think it is going to be a gift for mankind.

Hem Prakash Joshi
Chief HR Manager, Pfizer Animal Health India Ltd

WINNING *is* EVERYTHING

A 10-Step Guide *for* SURE SHOT SUCCESS

Deepak Behl

STERLING PAPERBACKS
An imprint of
Sterling Publishers (P) Ltd.
A-59, Okhla Industrial Area, Phase-II, New Delhi-110020.
Tel: 26387070, 26386209; Fax: 91-11-26383788
E-mail: mail@sterlingpublishers.com
www.sterlingpublishers.com

Winning is Everything
© 2012, Deepak Behl

Illustrations
© Sterling Publishers Pvt. Ltd.
ISBN 978 81 207 7358 5

All rights are reserved.
No part of this publication may be reproduced, stored in a retrieval system or transmitted, in any form or by any means, mechanical, photocopying, recording or otherwise, without prior written permission of the publisher.

Printed in India
Printed and Published by Sterling Publishers Pvt. Ltd., New Delhi-110 020.

FOREWORD

It gives me immense pleasure to introduce Mr. DEEPAK BEHL, my colleague in the field of HR and management teachers fraternity, as an effective author of an amazing self-help book, 'Winning is Everything'.

As an author with practical approach, he has very intelligently divided the subject into chapters covering all the requisite abilities essential for achieving success by students and junior & middle level managers in the corporate world.

He has not only touched the 'what' part of challenge, but has very lucidly handled the 'how' as well. I have personally liked the book very much, especially the chapters on Attitude, Skills, Leadership and Communication. The best part of the book is simple easily comprehensible language and smooth flow of thoughts in a very effective and coherent manner with suitable examples and interesting short stories.

I am convinced that all readers will be delighted to read, absorb, reflect and adopt some magic mantras, if not all, which he has very beautifully put across.

I wish Deepak all the best for this smart endeavour and quit sure that this book has all the required qualities to become one of the best sellers sooner than later.

Wishing 'Winning is everything' all the good luck!

Prof. Col. P.S. Bajaj
Ex-Chairman – IMT (DLP)
Senior Professor, IIPM
Executive Chairman, TUNE

DEDICATION

I dedicate my book to
my parents
for whom I was, am and will be indebted for ever...

My Mother – Late Smt. Sudarshan Behl
Who is not in this materialistic world to see my –
'self help book',
which I think will justify her
philosophy of life of helping everyone in need,
she will be my teacher for ever.

&

My idol - my Father – Sh. Sudarshan Lal Behl
Who runs his NGO – "Students' Bright Future Organisation"
and has played a pivotal role in making me strong enough to
help others and taught me to justify the name he has given
Deepak – who give light to others.

ACKNOWLEDGEMENTS

I learnt everything from you all only and sharing everything with you all, at many places I have mentioned about the individuals who, in my life - helped me, supported me, taught me, hand holded me and helped me in understanding some concepts of life which led towards 'Winning' but at many placed inadvertently I must have forgotten to mention some names of the people who taught me something somewhere, I apologise and promise to mention it in next edition if reminded in time.

'Deepak' has got no value without his –Jyoti (my wife), who sacrificed many hours, days and probably years, holding the fort behind me so that I can achieve my goals, not only this book but nothing was possible without her silent support and dedication, the credit goes to her.

There are others those who are in extended family (I believe in Krishna's – "Vasudev Kutumbakam") who made me whatever I am, starting with Ram Sir, my Guru, friend and philosopher, whose aim of life is to help everyone, taught me, supported me and guided me to 'take' the pleasure in 'giving'.

Prof. (Col.) P. S. Bajaj, Ex Chairman - IMT, was my mentor not only for my MBA studies but for the Management of Life. Mr. Sachdeva, Dogra ji, Negi ji, Mr. Deepak Singh, Atul Gaur, Parminder Kumar, Shilini Madam, Pushpinder Saluja, Dr. Manoj and everyone at IMT was a big support.

My cousin Rohit Manchanda, for whom I am the 'Ideal' wanted to make me an Ideal for the world, he also inspired me to wright the book, which should help all the success seekers.

Deepak Mendiratta, the knowledge bank, who met me during the beginning of my second career in Corporate World (After resigning from Police), introduced some modern management concepts like NLP (Neuro Linguistic Programming) and challenged me to face the world head on.

Prof. S C Kapoor, who always inspired me to guide others, is one of my teachers who should be given due credit and acknowledgement along with Prof. Sumit Chaudhary, they are 'Guru Drons' to me.

If I need to take a name of the magician who converted me from a student to 'Police Officer' can none other than Mr. Kali Ram Sharma, Ex. - Dy. Inspector General of Police – CRPF, he is one the most respected person in my life who laid the foundation of being gentleman officer.

Many more people including my seniors Maj Pratap Singh, Wg. Cdr. S. L. Soni, Subir Vyas, Stephen Magor and Julian Ayers shaped me for future challenges, my colleagues (Comdt. DPS Rana, Cdr. S M Kumar, Ranjeeka Sachdev, Anjali Ahuja, Manoj Arora, Amita Chanana, Kshitij Deopujari, Pankaj Bhola, Kamal Rana, Nivedita Awasthy, Abhishek Sadhu, Sanjay Keswani, Davinder Juj, Vikas Sharma and many more) helped me in learning stories for this book but the major contribution was from my colleagues (Nrapender, Sumit, Mahender, Suparna, Amit Caroli, Aradhana Dubey, Anil Miglani, Shiv Mehta, Ekta, Rajat Mankad and Shilpa Jhamb) helped me in managing the Corporate workload.

The blessing of Late Sh. Bhagwan Das Bhatia (Baba Ji) and Smt. Kako Masi (Amma Ji) were always with me.

Personal friends who became mentors included Hem Prakash Joshi, Dr. Hitender Setia, Manoj Karhuria, Vikrant Kaushal, Ashish Broota, Ashish Sikka, Uma Shankar - Archana Chauhan Kaushik, Mamta & Gaurav Rana, Meeta and Manish Nanda, Kavita and Sudeep Jairath, Monika and Rajesh, Monika and Bunty were always with us in the journey of life.

Many more people in this world I could not mention here helped me, this book is dedicated to them all as a gift of my love and affection.

And last but not the least a very special thanks to Sterling Publishers and Diamond Books for guiding, helping and publishing my book.

PREFACE

This is a Story of a Boatman who owned a small boat of 20 passengers capacity and his livelihood was to take people across the river and bring them back, one fine sunny day when he stated work he could get about 15 passengers for his first trip, he started calling and inviting people in high pitch of voice by saying - "Rs. 10 only, Rs. 10 only, hurry up only 5 seats left, no boat after this for an hour, hurry, just pay 10 and get across".

Few came and occupied vacant seats, few looked towards Boatman in the hope of reducing the rates further. Boatman observed a 'Saint' standing on the Bank of the River looking probably to cross the river but was not coming towards boat, the Boatman thought that he is a 'Saint', may not be making a lot of money and must be feeling difficult to pay Rs. 10 for crossing this small river. The Boatman approached the Saint and whispered – "for you who preach the world, I will charge only Rs. 5, hurry up, there is no boat for next one hour", the Saint smiled but did not utter anything, the Boatman was surprised but was convinced that he can fill up the vacant seats in Boat, he again whispered – "OK, I understand, you can only pay Rs. 2, hurry up come along, there is no boat for next one hour, why to waste time in waiting, I will manage in Rs. 2 only, occupy seat as early as possible, only 2 seats are left, join me, hurry up", but to the surprise of the Boatman" there was no impact on Saint, he kept on smiling and did not even reply.

Boatman, confused and surprised returned to the boat and as soon as he started, he saw something which was beyond his level of imagination, not only the Boatman but all the passengers were also amazed to see the Saint.

By now Boatman was quite clear why Saint did not reply to Boatman's request, he could also decipher why the Saint waited the boat to start and why he started crossing the river by walking on the water - the reason was simple and clear, he wanted to show others that he can walk on the water.

The Boatman shouted "wow, so you can walk on water and that is why you were not coming to my boat, can you please share how many years you took in learning this art.

Saint replied "20 years it took, I left my home, my family and my village, went to dense forests and spent 20 years day and night practicing this art".

The Boatman laughed loudly and said – "you have wasted 20 years of your precious life, what you could do is only useful for you and not for any other person on earth, only you can cross this river but you cannot help anybody". Look at me, I am not only making my livelihood with this small boat but helping many others in not only crossing the river but helping them in going for their work, it took me 20 days to build the boat and to learn the art of rowing, I am not only helping myself but many others as well in the journey of life, when I die, somebody else will be able to use this boat to help others but when you die, no one will have your abilities to help others and those will go with you.

The story ends here with a very logical question – are we like that Saint who spent years learning some art and want to take all with him when he die or we want to give something back to the society we have learnt many things from.

Now when I thought should my abilities and knowledge can be helpful for others or will these go with me, I decided to be a 'Boatman' instead of a 'Saint', whose abilities will be for everyone forever and I decided to pen down something which can help many in winning and making their life more liveable, enjoyable and successful.

Let us make this world a beautiful place to live and enjoy our lives...

CONTENTS

Foreword — xi
Acknowledgements — xiii
Preface — xv

1. Magic Mantras — 1
2. Attitude Decides Altitudes — 25
3. Skilled Abilities — 48
4. Inculcating Productive Habits — 79
5. Lead to Succeed — 103
6. Decide not to Perish — 128
7. Communicate Like Crazy — 142
8. Team (Together Everyone Achieves More) — 162
9. Motivation for a New 'You' — 188
10. The Spiritual Spirit — 205

MAGIC MANTRAS

(Tools to Start Succeeding)

Winners do different things, normal things are done by normal people.

We all know the phenomenon of appreciation and depreciation, Land and Property appreciate and Cars, Machines and other assets depreciate with time.

Do Human Beings Appreciate or Depreciate ?

What do you think, do human beings appreciate or depreciate, before reading the answer below, try to give the answer yourself...

The answer is that **human beings with positive and learning attitude -- appreciate and the ones with negative attitude -- depreciate.**

You should further read this book if you want to understand the process of appreciation which is discussed in a systematic step by step approach with the help of many interesting stories and examples with a lot of learning.

Let us start with some basic concepts.

You Know that You Know

Here is an interesting question for you all:

Please consider the following circle as the circle of 'whole knowledge of the world'.

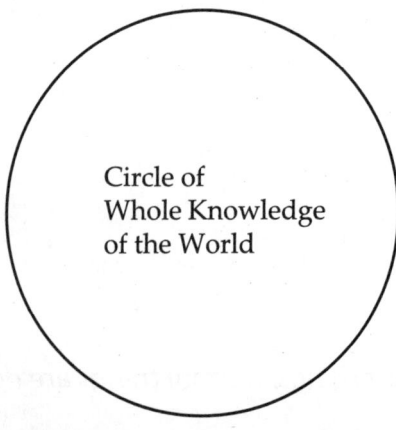

Now the question is - what is your level of knowledge? Try spotting your level on this circle :

Before answering this question let us accept that we all generally know 3 to 4 languages only out of thousands of languages in the world. We only know about few foods out of lakhs of cuisines. Our knowledge of beverages is also very limited, how many cities and capitals can we spot on the world map. How much do we know about rocket science, nuclear sciences, mechanical science, social sciences, behavioural sciences, electronics, computers, IT, history, geography, mathematics, biology, physics, chemistry, commerce, accountancy, economics, etc.

Probably most of us will just put a dot on this circle as we know that we know a little, to be very specific - very little.

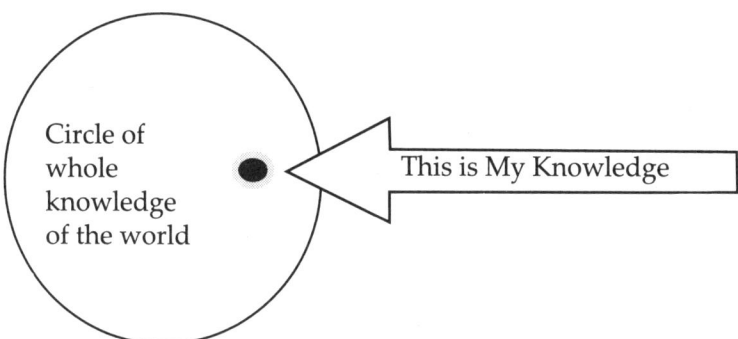

Now to understand this concept, in place of a dot let us allocate a 'pie' (marked black) in the circle of our knowledge below :

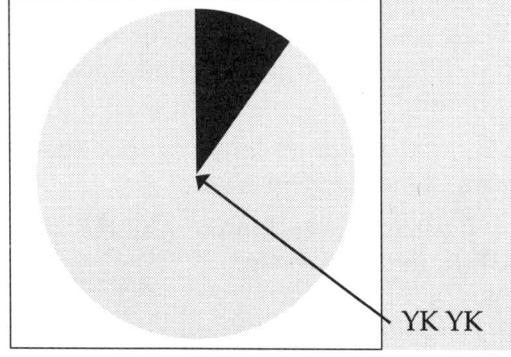

This black portion is YK YK (You Know that You Know), we know that we know a little that is why a small pie is given to this segment, if I ask you to give some examples from this segment you can say that :

I know that I can read and understand English.

I know my name, where is my house and basic geography, history, maths, science, etc.

I know I like Indian food and know how it is cooked.

I know why planes fly, how boats float in water and why the heart beats.

But we also know that we don't know quite a lot of things, if we need to plot this segment on the same circle, it will look like the following one :

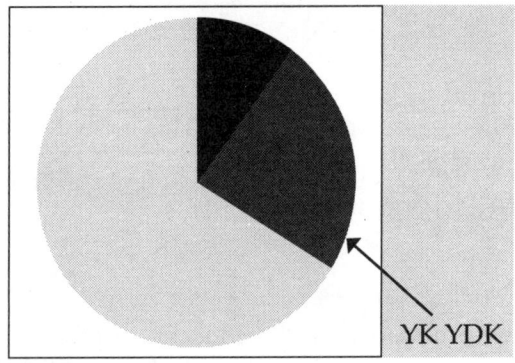

Where the grey portion shows the YK YDK (You Know that You Don't Know) area which is much bigger than the first one and now if I ask you to give me some examples for this segment you will say :

I know that I don't know how to speak languages like German, Chinese and Spanish.

I know that there are Moroccan and Mexican foods but don't know how these are cooked.

Magic Mantras 5

I know that Amsterdam and Maimi do exist in the world, where exactly, I don't know.

I know pilots can fly planes but I don't know how to fly them.

Now the main question is the rest of the portion (light grey) in the following circle, what does that show... try answering.

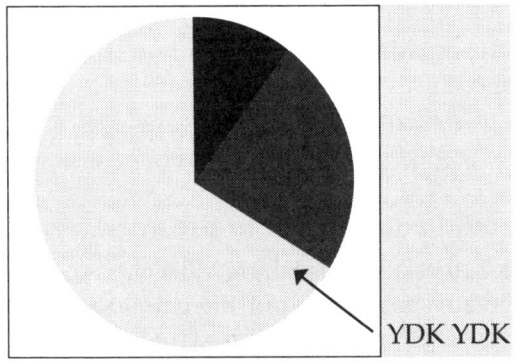

This portion shows YDK YDK (You Don't Know that You Don't Know).

Think over it and try to give some examples for this segment...

You actually **cannot** give any examples from this segment because you yourself don't know that you don't know and if you try to quote any example, it will fall in the category of 'You Know that You Don't Know'.

{ *'Always' and 'Never' are two words in Management you should 'Always' remember 'Never' to use them.* }

We will be discussing many things in this book which will fall in the category of YK YK (You know that you know) and may be a repetition for you, many things may fall in YK YDK (You know that you don't know) and now will be the chance for you to grab those for rest of your life, and some will surely fall in the category of YDK – YDK, you need to give a lot of attention on these points, find it out from the book, read it, understand it, learn to practise it, I can bet and challenge that these can turnaround the wheel of your life and bring you closer to success.

This book is full of examples, stories and management lessons, which are not only based on my experiences and personal researches of many years but are also the outcome of the experiences of many successful and happy corporate honchos, management professionals and trainers.

To proceed further let us see another concept-

What should you become in life

During last 10 years while taking MBA classes, I have faced this question many times, most of the students even after taking admission in MBA are still confused for their selection of career, the best action you can take is to –

> *Convert your Passion into Profession for Sure Shot Success.*

You should become what you dream to be, where your passion lies and what you will feel doing not only good but great in life. Do not pick up a career only because your parents advised you to do so or someone observed others to be successful in that stream or you think you can make more money in that profession, without any interest in a particular field, it is just impossible to be successful if you do not love your profession.

> *A right person for the right job at the right time on the right salary is the right formula.*

But putting these 'Rights' is always a challenge, let us see the practical side of this :

> *If you are not picked up for a Job – You may be too smart for that job*

As a management professional, I have played the role of a career counsellor also and have taken many sessions with junior/middle level managers in many business schools. I have come across some de-motivated individuals also who could not get selected in their dream jobs because they could not clear interviews and started believing that they are not smart enough or not capable that is why they were 'rejected' by the top MNCs / top class Indian brands.

I do not accept that they were 'rejected', rather they were not picked up because probably they did not 'meet the criteria' or they were 'too smart' for the jobs offered.

Common Reasons of Non-Selection (we should not use the word – Rejection)

- **Inappropriate Job Application**

Job applications and resumes are your first impression and an inappropriate job application can close the chapter even before it is opened. If you are not very sure about the application, show it to a professional or HR expert for right advice.

- **Non-Professional Resume**

I have seen thousands of resumes and have found that some applicants spoil their impression because of bad layout, unattractive looks or sometimes multicoloured resumes, spelling/grammar mistakes, wrong description in job profile, inflated achievements, copied contents or objective statements, length of resume – too short or too long, quality of printing and paper, professional presentation, non-visibility of salient achievements or points, etc. One should take care of all these points to make sure that you cross the first hurdle to be called for a personal interview and once you are called the game may entirely change. I have met some very good candidates with bad resumes and also some very bad candidates with good resumes.

Some important sections apart from your qualification, experience, achievements, job profile is the personal data which includes your hobbies and interest in games and sports, extra curricular activities which clarify your ability to de-stress, lead, command and overall smartness as a balanced personality.

- **Resume Fraud (how ethical it is)**

It will be interesting to know that 90 % applicants do big or small resume frauds, although rest 10 % never get a job.

How ethical it is to do a resume fraud is the question I have loved to answer in many Companies, Business Schools, Seminars and Conferences. We do understand candidates do not wish to give step by step record of their career, specially they do not want to mention the companies they worked for a litter while, either the candidate or the companies did not like each other and that is why they moved very quickly.

In Hindi we say *'Aate me Thora Namak Chalega Lekin Namak me Aata Nahi'* (some salt will work in flour but not flour in salt), similarly the little hidings can be considered acceptable in resumes but not the hiding of pertinent facts, if you have shown yourself as a VP and you were a Manager – it is a fraud and not a mistake and of course no employer will ever think of considering you for any responsible senior level position.

- **Slipping in GDs (Group Discussions)**

If you need to appear in a GD, never think that you will be picked up if you shout and make others listen to you, what you speak, how you speak and when you speak is the judging criteria. Your knowledge, communication and presentation will decide your selection. If you know the topic fully, you can take a lead to start the discussion, you will get some consideration

Magic Mantras

for this lead also, otherwise you can contribute in between. Speaking continuously or keeping mum to wait for your turn also may go against you, if someone supports you, you should thank him and after contributing, give others chance to put their point of view also. But if someone criticises you, recognise it and give your explanation, if you are at mistake, there is no harm in accepting it by feeling sorry.

> *An arrow can be sent only by pulling it back, so when life is dragging you back with difficulties it means that its going to launch you towards victory.*

Now the question is what will happen if you just know nothing about the subject in GD, the solution is to listen first the knowledgeable participants and then paraphrasing the outcome in more impressive and selective words, this is known as smart and quick learning.

- **Dodging the Interviewers**

Interview means "internal views", the more you attend the more you become confident to face it. Be truthful and sincere in your efforts, you should be looking interested for the job you are applying for but should not show that you are dying for it.

Example : If interviewers ask you - if you can put some extra efforts and time to justify the role, always say yes and be willing to put some extra efforts and time to be contributive for the cause but if they expect you to spend 12 hours a day for the job, you need to softly say no by giving reasons how this will not help the company in achieving the goals and how this will not match with your long-term plan of staying with the company, This will also give the impression to the interviewers that you are the person who can take decisions and can distinguish between right and wrong, this will make your candidature even stronger.

> *You do not lose because of failure; you lose much prior to that with the fear of failure*

The interviews can be of any type like - Group Interviews (taken by a group of interviewers from different backgrounds), Stressed Interviews (to create stress to check how you perform under stressful conditions), Informal Interviews (where you are judged in the most natural way), Psychological Interviews (when you are required to be checked psychologically for certain types of role like in Police or Army, etc.), Structured Interviews (in which all the questions are structured and preset to be compared with answers by other candidates) and Non-Structured Interviews (where no pre fixed pattern is used but the internal view of the abilities to perform a particular job and suitability to the role is checked and matched in a natural manner).

- **Not Understanding Business Games**

This is relatively a new phenomenon in India where many companies have started expecting the applicants to participate in playing some psychological or business games, where the basic traits of the applicants can be crystal clear and they can't hide or suppress the natural tendencies in handling and dealing with different situations. The most common output is knowing if the candidate is a good team player, if he is motivated, can motivate others, can think strategically, can manage others in an efficient and effective manner and can lead and plan well or not.

- **Bad Appearance and Presentation**

The confident appearance adds to your level of seriousness for the role you are being interviewed. You should give special attention to your physical appearance and appear properly dressed up in sober colours.

A strict no for males is cigarette or *pan masala* odour, and for females is heavy makeup and inappropriate clothes, dark nail enamels, dark lipstick shades, etc. You should wear a decent footwear.

Personal hygiene plays a critical role and how do you smell, look and sound are three very important areas which are indirectly responsible to make your impression. One should use good deodorants, perfumes, aftershaves, talcum powders and sprays but overdoing anything should always be restrained.

- **Not Adhering to Manners and Courtesies**

How you behave in an interview decides your chances of being selected, there is always a basic standard of manners and courtesies associated with all the job roles, the higher you go, the more these are required. For example you may be asked for tea / coffee either in the waiting room or in the interview room and if a plate of biscuits is offered with tea, it will be noticed how many do you pick up, the maximum limit is always one that too if there are sufficient numbers left for all others to share, say if there are 5 candidates and 4 biscuits, you should pick up just a half to make sure that there is one for everyone. Never criticise for any administrative or logical arrangements, it shows your poor and negative side of character.

Many people think that not agreeing with interviewers may be one of the cause of their rejection, which may not be always right, you can disagree with the interviewers but in the right manner. Sometimes the interviewers intentionally create such situations, where you need to disagree with them, this is done by them to check your abilities to call a spade a spade.

How to Disagree with the Interviewers

You need to remain on the ethical side and should call a spade a spade, if you do not know the answer of any question, accept it graciously, never try to dodge or give wrong information but when you know the right answer, you need to disagree with the interviewers politely. The best way to do it is to tell the interviewers that they may be right as they are more experienced but what you think is this....

Saying interviewers that they don't know, or they are telling a lie or disrespecting them for their lack of knowledge should never take place. This can be one of the techniques to put you in a stressful situation as this may be a stress interview.

How to Prepare Yourself for Interviews

1. Never fake body language. Be yourself, do not pretend, originality always wins.
2. Be ready to introduce yourself, start the communication by wishing them first.
3. You should talk about your achievements however boasting should be avoided. If you don't know anything, feel sorry for not knowing it (you are not expected to know everything).
4. Be relaxed and frank but not casual.
5. Talk to all interviewers and use the same language in replying.
6. Make eye contact, smile and enjoy the challenge.
7. Never criticise (specially your present employer or current boss).
8. Be ready with a list of your positive points (5 to 7) and negative – maximum 3 with your action plan, how you work to get rid of them – the execution part.
9. Be ready to answer some **common questions** like
    a. 'Your introduction' and 'family background' (you should give your name, where you are born and brought up, from where did you do your schooling and education, your strong points, your aim of life but never give a lot of data, which is already mentioned in your resume, in family background the names of your family members are not required, interviewers need to know something different, state if you are from a business class family or a family of intellectuals).
    b. Your current job description and your achievements.
    c. Your aim (divided into short-term objectives)
    d. The reason of leaving current job / the thought of change.
    e. Where do you see yourself in next 5/ 10 years?

f. What do you know about the company you are applying for? (before going for interview, get to know everything may be from company website, their competitors, challenges they are facing and growth plans)
g. Your knowledge of the current affairs, politics, economy and business arena.
h. Happiest day / saddest day of your life.
i. Books you like or recently read / your favourite authors.
j. Movies you like or recently seen.
k. Technical questions related to your area of expertise.
l. How do you think you will be an asset for the company?

Should You Ask Questions From Interviewers

If given a chance - Yes, but only one or two sensible questions like what are the challenges of the role they are interviewing you for and when they describe, you can tell them how you have handled these situations in the past and how do you think you can handle these if given a chance, this will help you in making your candidature stronger.

Thank them and convey that if given a chance, you will go beyond their level of expectation to perform well. You should show eagerness to join but keep in mind that over eagerness may kill your chances.

You have got all the rights to meet your boss, share your views, listen to him, know him and then only take the decision.

Should You Have Many Degrees and Collect Many at Same Time

No, not required, specially more number of degrees at the same time questions your decision-making abilities and credibility of the courses you have done. No credit is given for this as you could not have done justice with any of the courses done together because you could not devote appropriate time for any one. The selection is not only on degrees or more degrees, it is always a right balance of experience, merit, level of smartness, pleasing personality, ability of decision-making and ability to disagree if required.

People generally take the help of their 'friends' to prepare for interviews and may ignore others' advice even if others possess more relevant knowledge of the subject matter. You can understand this with the following story :

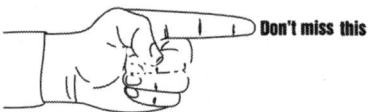
Don't miss this

A Smart Enemy is Better Than A Foolish Friend

Once upon a time there was a group of friends who decided to go to next state for business, they executed the plan, crossed the jungle, reached the other state, did very good business and earned a lot of cash.

While coming back to their state and before crossing the jungle they thought of their safety and security as they never wanted to take a lot of cash with them. While they were thinking what to do, someone named Raghu, who claimed to be a trader himself approached them and requested them to include him in their team for travelling through the jungle and explained that he is a regular traveller and do not wish to cross the jungle all alone. He also offered them help in crossing the jungle from the safest route, all the traders agreed and included him in their group.

This was a big mistake by the group of traders, they never knew that Raghu was actually a thief and joined them only to rob them, this was his modus operandi. When traders were deciding how to save their cash, Raghu advised them to take diamonds in lieu of cash and told them to wrap diamonds in a polythene and swallow them in such a manner so that they can vomit it back after reaching their state. Raghu advised that this way no one will ever come to know that they have hidden diamonds in their stomach.

Traders were impressed with this technique and thanked Raghu for such useful advice, they all bought diamonds against all the cash they earned, rapped them in a polythene in small quantities and swallowed them with water like a medicine tablet.

Raghu thought of killing them one by one en route to get the diamonds from their stomach and started the journey from jungle to the other state.

Magic Mantras

As luck would have it, when they were swallowing the diamonds, a parrot who was flying over them saw this and informed this to his friend, who was a notorious dacoit in the jungle. When the group of traders were crossing the jungle, they were caught by a gang of dacoits. They got very frightened but they were sure that dacoits will not be able to get anything out of them as they can never guess that the diamonds are hidden in their stomach.

When the group of traders were taken to the leader of the dacoits, the parrot started shouting – 'These people have diamonds, these people have diamonds'.

The dacoit asked the traders to give whatever they had, however traders showed their inability to give anything as they pretended not to have anything and asked the dacoit to frisk them thoroughly if he doesn't believe them.

Dacoit ordered some of his gang members to check and frisk the traders but nothing could be found. Raghu, the thief in trader's attire, who was guiding the traders' group for a safe route got surprised with this as it never happened on this route in the past, he was terrified but just kept mum.

The parrot again shouted – 'They have diamonds, they have diamonds'. The dacoit got quite surprised and got them frisked again but got nothing, he was annoyed on parrot for speaking a lie.

But the parrot was convinced with what it saw, it again shouted "They have got diamonds and they have hidden these in their stomach".

Now the dacoit got totally confused, he was not sure who is right - traders or parrot and decided to check this by cutting someone's stomach. All the traders got terrified and they knew if the dacoit gets the diamonds in any one's stomach, he will kill all of them to get all the diamonds. Raghu also got very much terrified and could see his death quite near, he knew that the dacoit will not listen to him if he says he is not from that group and in search of diamonds will tear his stomach apart for sure.

Once Raghu was convinced that he is going to die, he decided to help at least other traders, he volunteered to be the first to get killed and approached the dacoit and told him that the parrot is lying and they do not have any diamonds in their stomach. He offered the dacoit to cut his stomach to check this fact.

The group of traders got pleasantly surprised but were sad for Raghu as he was giving his life to save them all. The dacoit decided to cut off Raghu's stomach to check the diamonds and ordered his gang member to kill Raghu to check his stomach.

The gang members could not found any diamonds in Raghu's stomach who sacrificed his life to save many lives of traders, who started shedding tears on Raghu's sacrifice and requested dacoit to release them.

Dacoit was annoyed that he killed someone without any reason as there were no diamonds, why the parrot was saying that continuously, he got so annoyed with the parrot that he killed his parrot and asked his gang to release all the traders.

Traders thanked him, appreciated Raghu's sacrifice and ran towards their state.

Moral of the story:

1. An Intelligent enemy is better than a foolish friend, in this story, how Raghu, being an enemy also saved the life of other group members and how a foolish friend (dacoit) killed his own friend (parrot) in frustration.

2. Never lose your temperament in adverse situations, if you maintain your cool, you will be able to get some solution of the problem.

Self-Assessment

On the path of success, you need to assess yourself, you need to know your 'Strong Points' and 'Development Areas'(why to call these as weaknesses or shortcomings), you need to make your strong points as your strengths and need to work on your development areas to improve further.

Before we proceed further list your strong points here :

My strong points are :

1. ....
2. ....
3. ....

4. ....
5. ....

Make a plan how you can further improve on above points and how you will make them your strengths.

Now list down your 'Development Areas' :

1. ....
2. ....
3. ....

Now write down your plan to remove these weaknesses. What is the plan to remove them systematically? What steps you will take? What is the time limit, how will you measure your progress? Who are the people you can take help from and how will you take the help from them, if those people are busy or not able to help due to some reasons? What will you do, more you elaborate your plans, more sure you will be for your success, because the success of removing your shortcomings will give you enough strength to pursue bigger goals in your journey towards a successful life.

You need to take some drastic actions to be successful, the first and foremost action is to appoint 'Your Personal Board of Directors' who will guide you to perform better and better in life. There should be a minimum of 5 from different fields, one can be from your family may be your elder cousin (do not make someone your board of director if he / she loves you very much as love is blind and that is why they will not be able to see your weaknesses), others can be your teachers / mentors, boss, colleagues or anyone who is happy, positive and successful himself / herself.

> *If you love yourself then only others will and if you respect yourself then only others should.*

Second action you need to take is to **make a list of actions you need to take to be successful** and this book will surely help you out in achieving your goals by providing appropriate Knowledge, Attitude, Skills and Habits (**KASH** formula is described in details in first four chapters of this book).

Importance of Training and Development

Training and Development is a planned process to modify and improve **Knowledge, Attitude, Skills and Habits** (**KASH** formula) through learning experience to achieve effective performance.

Impression of Training in Some Organisations

We may discuss volumes about the importance of training and development for individuals and organisations to succeed but in some of the organisations, training is treated as an alternative to regular boring work or as an essential time wasting exercise which is futile, the following example of one of the IOM in a company can explain my point of view.

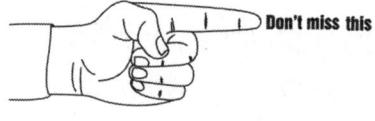
Don't miss this

S.H.I.T.

From: Vice President   To: All Employees

SUBJECT: SPECIAL HIGH INTENSITY TRAINING (SHIT)

In order to assure the highest levels of quality work and productivity from employees, it will be our policy to keep all employees well trained through our program of SPECIAL HIGH INTENSITY TRAINING (S.H.I.T.).

We are trying to give employees more S.H.I.T. than anyone else. If you feel that you do not receive your fair share of S.H.I.T. on the

Magic Mantras 19

job, please see your manager. You will be immediately placed at the top of the S.H.I.T. list, and our managers are especially skilled at seeing that you get all the S.H.I.T. you can handle.

Employees who don't take their S.H.I.T. will be placed in DEPARTMENTAL EMPLOYEE EVALUATION PROGRAMS (D.E.E.P S.H.I.T.) . Those who fail to take D.E.E.P. S.H.I.T. seriously will have to go to EMPLOYEE ATTITUDE TRAINING (E.A.T. S.H.I.T.). Since our managers took S.H.I.T. before they were promoted, they don't have to do S.H.I.T. anymore.

If you are full of S.H.I.T., you may be interested in job training others. We can add your name to our BASIC UNDERSTANDING LECTURE LIST (B.U.L.L S.H.I.T.). Those who are full of B.U.L.L S.H.I.T. will get the S.H.I.T. jobs and can apply for promotion to DIRECTOR OF INTENSITY PROGRAMMING (D.I.P. S.H.I.T.).

If you have any further questions, please direct them to our HEAD OF TRAINING, SPECIAL HIGH INTENSITY TRAINING (H.O.T S.H.I.T.).

Thank you,

BOSS IN GENERAL
SPECIAL HIGH INTENSITY TRAINING
(B.I.G. S.H.I.T.)

Difference between Activity and Process

This has been a topic of choice for me to explain in many Business / Hotel Management Colleges.

Understanding the difference between the activity and process will solve a lot of our problems, the positive results are sometimes away from us despite your best efforts because we perform some processes in the activity manner.

Activity is one time action and process is a continuation, summation or combination of similar or different types of activities...

Just to check if you have understood the above statement, let me ask you a question :

Eating food is what - an activity or a process.....

Take a minute to answer

Do not look beneath for the answer, try yourself...

The right answer is – Eating food is a process which you should keep on doing thrice a day for your life time to keep your body moving, even if you are on fast for one or two days the process continues with a pause and does not end upto your life span.

Now the question is how the concept of Activity and Process will help you out...

If you understand the concept you will start asking this question from yourself in many situations, for an example when you are motivating your team, you should ask this question to yourself if motivation is an activity (only one time action) or a process (which continues) the answer is that motivation is a process and it will be effective only when you accept and implement it like a process, you keep on motivating your team thrice a day (just like eating food), then only the motivation will show its magic.

If we do not understand the difference and keep on performing some important processes like one time activity the positive results may not come, this is also true in Learning, Decision Making, Building Habits, Changing Attitude, Communicating, Building Teams, Bringing Change, Sharpening Abilities, Honing Skills, Becoming Emotionally Intelligent or Spiritually Intelligent as all these are processes and not activities and are only effective if these are performed as processes.

Keep processing...

Smart Work V/s Hard Work

There is always a question if one should become a hard worker or smart worker, young managers are always curious to know what is hard work and what is smart work, they want to know the difference and the technique to shift from hard work to smart work, I am sure you will learn a smart lesson from the below mentioned story.

Magic Mantras 21

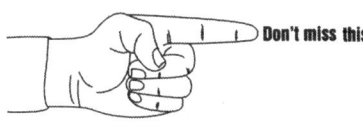

The Smart Move

An Indian walks into a bank in New York City and asks for the loan officer. He tells the loan officer that he is going to India on business for two weeks and needs to borrow $5,000.

The bank officer tells him that the bank will need some form of security for the loan, so the Indian hands over the keys and documents of his Ferrari parked on the street in front of the bank. The loan officer agrees to accept the car as collateral for the loan.

The bank's president and its officers all enjoy a good laugh at the Indian for using a $250,000 Ferrari as collateral against a $5,000 loan. An employee of the bank then drives the Ferrari into the bank's underground garage and parks it there.

Two weeks later, the Indian returns, repays the $5,000 and the interest, which comes to $15.41.

The loan officer says, "Sir, we are very happy to have had your business, and this transaction has worked out very nicely, but we are a little puzzled.

While you were away, we checked you out and found that you are a multi-millionaire. What puzzles us is, why would you bother to borrow "$5,000"?

The Indian replies:

"Where else in New York City can I park my car for two weeks for only $15.41 and expect it to be there when I return"

Let me explain the phenomenon of smart work in bit more details by an example :

Just imagine you have been given a task to roll away a huge big rock much bigger and heavier than you, how will you do it? :

Suggest me your line of action and write them here in the given space below :

1. I can try to push it with full strength to roll it away.
2. I can bring some ropes to pull it to other side.

3. I can bring a hammer to break it into pieces to get it removed from the place.
4. I can do ....(write what you can do to move it further.)
5. ....(any other action)
6. ....(any helping tools required)

You all know that it is a tough challenge and cannot be done by hard work, the probable solution will come out from smart work only:

You just need to arrange an iron rod of about your length and a small stone to be placed near the rock and do the following action to get the huge rock roll out of your way :

Now see carefully the big rock in the picture is your 'Problem' (which is looking quite big to you), the iron rod is your 'Ability' which you will apply to remove your problem and the small rock which will work as a catalyst is your 'Motivation.'

 **If your Father is a Poor man, it is your fate but if your Father-in-Law is a Poor man, it is your fault.**

OK, now on a serious note – is the hard work (or smart work) in your hand – Yes, it is. You can increase or decrease the inputs as per the situation. Is the luck in your hand – some say no, but I say yes, it is in your hands but indirectly... how ?

Magic Mantras 23

With the help of smart work, we can increase the portion of luck in our lives, let me prove this by the following example :

If one dreams that one day some industrialist will come to him to invite him to join in as one of the board of directors in his company, it may sound foolish and remain in dreams only but if one works smart, makes his mark, increases his knowledge, sharpens his skills, communicates effectively, participates in seminars and conferences, gives lectures on the topic of his expertise, covered by media and if he is *'Googlable'*, he will reach on such a position that in seminars industrialists will come up to him and ask him to join their company as a board of director because he is an authority in his subject. He will be considered lucky, because now it is possible for him to be called by an industrialist, now people will actually call him lucky.

Some people say Sachin Tendulkar is lucky to have his Ferrari, but just think how hard working he is. He has scored his centuries first and then he has became lucky by his hard work, can you imagine who much efforts he has put in making 100 centuries (He is at 99 at present, I am sure by the time this book is out on stands for sale, he will cross 100, we wish him good luck...)

Management Lesson
Being Oversmart

A shepherd was herding his flock in a remote pasture when suddenly a brand-new BMW advanced out of the dust cloud towards him. The driver, a young man in an Armani suit, Gucci shoes, Ray Ban sunglasses and Versace tie, leaned out the window and asked the shepherd, "If I tell you exactly how many sheep you have in your flock, will you give me one?" The shepherd looked at the man, obviously a yuppie, then looked at his peacefully-grazing flock and calmly answered, "Sure." The yuppie parked his car, whipped out his notebook and connected it to a cell phone, then he surfed to a NASA page on the internet where he called up a GPS satellite navigation system, scanned the area, and then opened up a database and an Excel spreadsheet with complex formulas. He sent an email on his Blackberry and after a few minutes, received a response. Finally, he prints out a 150 page report on his hi-tech, miniaturized printer then turns to the shepherd and says, "You have exactly 1586 sheep." "That is correct; take one of the sheep", said the shepherd. He watches the young man select one of the animals and bundle it into his car. Then the shepherd says: "If I can tell you exactly what your business is, will you give me back my sheep?" "OK, why not." answered the young man. "Clearly, you are a Management Consultant who is Six Sigma Black Belt," said the shepherd.

"That's correct," says the yuppie, "but how did you guess that?" "No guessing required." answers the shepherd. "You turned up here although nobody called you. You want to get paid for an answer I already knew, to a question I never asked, and you don't know crap about my business. Now give me back my dog."

Lesson: Being Smart is a Blessing and being Over Smart is a Curse...

If we are born to help others,
why the hell others are born for.

ATTITUDE DECIDES ALTITUDES

(The Foundation Stone of Success)

If an egg is broken from outside a life ends, but if it is broken from inside, a life begins...

Before we start this very interesting, informative and life changing chapter, let us play a game to solve a riddle together, this will help you out in understanding this chapter in its right spirit and you will benefit a lot with it.

You need to solve a riddle and promise me not to see the answers on the following pages.

The riddle is very simple, the following are a group of 9 equidistant dots :

Join all these 9 equidistant dots:

1) with **5** straight lines
2) without lifting your pen/pencil
3) and without over-writing.

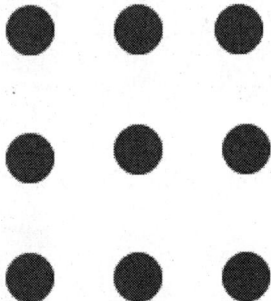

You solve the riddle in the mean time let me share a small but real story about a customer of a motor company and its customer-care executive.

A complaint was received by the customer care department of a motor company:

"This is the second time I am writing to you, and I don't blame you for not answering me, because I sounded crazy earlier, but it is a fact that we have a tradition in our family of ice cream for dessert after dinner each night. But the flavour of ice cream varies, so every night, after we've taken the dinner, the whole family votes on which flavour of ice cream we should have and I drive down to the store to get it. It's also a fact that I recently purchased a new car from your company and since then my trips to the store have created a problem. You see, every time I buy a vanilla ice cream, when I start back from the store my car won't start. If I get any other ice cream, the car starts just fine.

Attitude Decides Altitudes

I want you to know I'm serious about this question, no matter how silly it sounds: "What is there about this car that makes it not start when I get vanilla ice cream, and easy to start whenever I get any other kind?"

The motor car company president was understandably sceptical about the letter, but sent an engineer to check it out anyway. The latter was surprised to be greeted by a successful, obviously well educated man in a fine neighbourhood. Engineer had arranged to meet the man just after dinner, so the two hopped into the car and drove to the ice cream store. It was vanilla ice cream that night and, sure enough, after they came back to the car, it wouldn't start. The engineer returned for three more nights.

(by this time you must have solved the riddle, the story will continue after the riddle discussion)

Now before we proceed further, let us see the solution of the riddle :

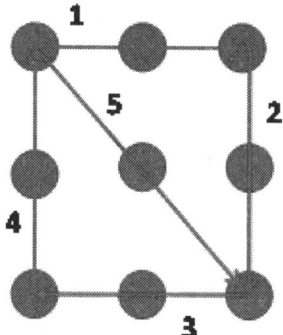

Some of you must be happy to solve it before looking for an answer and would have said – such a simple riddle, everyone can solve it, but some of you must have faced problems in getting the right answer and some of you could not have solved this at all. Where is the perception playing its role, I will explain a little bit later but just want to tell you that I just played a trick with you by not asking the real riddle, it was just a joke, but this joke also teaches a lesson that sometimes we treat no challenges or small challenges as big challenges and fear to solve them or leave them unsolved, the actual riddle you need to solve is as follows :

Join all 9 equidistant dots:
1) with **4** straight lines
2) without lifting your pen/pencil
3) and without over-writing.

(Please note, this time the maximum straight lines you can draw are 4 only)

Meanwhile you solve the problem, let us continue with our story...

The first night, they got chocolate. The car started. The second night, they got strawberry. The car started. The third night they ordered vanilla. The car failed to start. Now the engineer, being a logical man, refused to believe that this man's car was allergic to vanilla ice cream.

He therefore arranged, to continue his visits for as long as it took to solve the problem. And towards the end he began to take notes: he jotted down all sorts of data: time of day, type of gas uses, time to drive back and forth, etc. In a short time, he had a clue: the man took less time to buy vanilla than any other flavour. Why? The answer was in the layout of the store. Vanilla, being the most popular flavour, was in a separate case at the front of the store for quick pickup. All the other flavours were kept in the back of the store at a different counter where it took considerably longer to check out the flavour. Now, the question for the engineer was why the car wouldn't start when it took less time.

Once time became problem - not the vanilla ice cream, the engineer quickly came up with the answer: "Vapour lock". It was happening every night; but the extra time taken to get the other flavours allowed the engine to cool down sufficiently to start. When the man got vanilla, the engine was still too hot for the vapour lock to dissipate.

Remember: Even crazy looking problems are sometimes real and all problems seem to be simple only when we find the solution with a cool and balanced attitude.

{ *Don't just say its "IMPOSSIBLE" without putting a sincere effort...Observe the word "IMPOSSIBLE" carefully... You can see "I'M' POSSIBLE"...* }

Attitude Decides Altitudes

What really matters is your attitude and your perception with the balanced approach. Somebody has said rightly that "Don't cry when the sun is gone, because the tears won't let you see the stars."

By the way...did you solve the riddle with 4 straight lines without lifting your pen and without overwriting, if yes very good Congratulations..., if no, please see the solutions below :

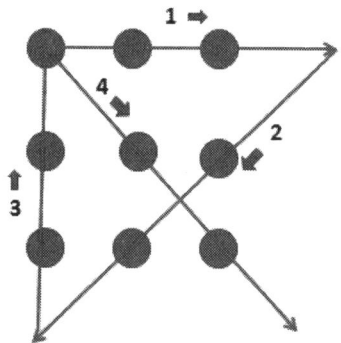

After seeing the solution, it seems, how easy it was, you just need to break the attitude of keeping yourself in an invisible box in and around the dots, think beyond the box (we call it **out of the box thinking**), go beyond the limits 'You have set for Yourself' and you get the answer. If you have solved this riddle, you are really a genius and if you want to check if you are a super genius, then you need to solve it further on the following conditions :

Join all 9 equidistant dots :
1) with **3** straight lines
2) without lifting your pen/pencil
3) and without over-writing.

(Please note, this time the maximum straight lines you can draw are 3 only)

The base of your attitude is your perception, if you are able to mould your perception, your attitude will automatically change, before proceeding further, let us understand perception first.

PERCEPTION

A process, by which individuals organize and interpret their sensory impressions in order to give meaning to their environment, is known as perception.

Before proceeding further, I just wanted to check if you have solved the riddle, if yes Congrats again– you are a super genius and if no, here is the solution :

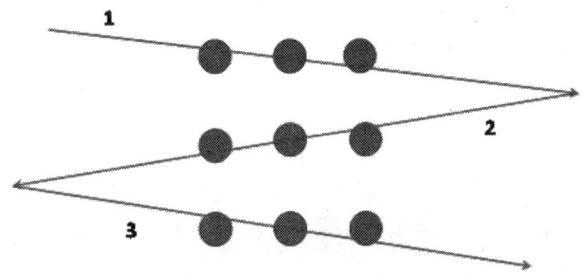

I am sure initially you must have thought that this is not possible, how can one join 9 dots with 4 straight lines and if at all it was possible, how someone can join 9 dots with 3 straight lines, but your perception kept on changing and you kept on believing that it can be done and it is possible.

Before we proceed further on the learning for riddle, can you try to join all 9 dots with one line, and this time at-least don't say - not possible as by this time you have learnt to change your attitude from 'IMPOSSIBLE to I M POSSIBLE'.

I am sure you must have solved the riddle by now, here is the solution otherwise, if you solved it yourself, Congratulations, you are a super duper genius:

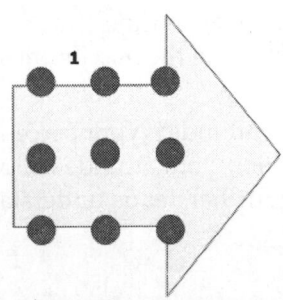

Attitude Decides Altitudes

The only thing you need to keep in mind while solving this riddle this time is that the pen / line should be so thick that it touches all points just in one stroke, the learning here is to make your abilities so strong that they solve the problems of your life just in one stroke. My aim and dream behind writing this book is that only, if you are successful after reading this book, I will feel happy and will feel as if I have achieved my aim in life. Do write me back, I will share your success stories with millions and billions.

How Perception is Formed

The first and foremost factor which influences the perception is the individual himself. The attitude, motive, interest, expectations, experience, knowledge, background, thinking, IQ & EQ level, the knowledge of the subject, etc. are the reasons which influence an individual in understanding, interpreting and giving meaning to his / her surroundings. The object is the second important aspect which may change the perception of the individual completely. Basically novelty, motion, sound, size, background and proximity are the main factors of object. Have you observed that the rates of coloured advertisements are higher in comparison to the black and white ones? Have you also observed that the big hoardings are more likely to be observed than the small ones? The moving objects are noticed over the stationary ones and the inclination / interest towards the object is another factor influencing perception. When we go to the market, we are able to see the shops where we wanted to shop (because of interest) and just overlook all other things. If someone asks us about the sale offers in other shops, we won't be able to tell about that probably because of the interest in objects of our desire.

Let us see an example from the following story of two monks and their different perceptions :

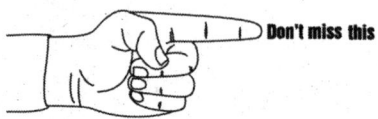

The Story of Two Monks

This is the story from Tibet, there lived two young monks, one day they were going to a distant place, en route they came across a deep river, when they were about to cross it, a young lady approached them and requested them to help her in crossing the river.

Monks, who were instructed by their preacher to remain away from females got quite confused if they should help her and even talk to her. They still asked the lady how they can help her in crossing the river, the lady told them that she does not knew how to swim and requested one of the monks to carry her on his back to cross the river as she was not tall enough to cross the deep river.

Where first monk politely refused to help her, the second one was ready to pick her up on his back to cross the river, he crossed the river carrying the women on his back, lady thanked him and went on her way.

The first monk who refused her to help as he was not expected to touch her while helping her was very annoyed with the second monk and did not talk to him for the whole day. Next day also he could not forgive the second monk, who not only touched a female but even carried her on his back.

Attitude Decides Altitudes

The second monk who helped the lady forgot the incident after helping and concentrated in his meditation but the first monk who could not forgive him was not able to meditate because of his anger.

When the second monk who helped the lady asked first monk about the reason of him not concentrating in meditation, the first monk angrily told him about first monk's misdeed and cursed him for touching and carrying a women on his back.

The first monk replied, "I have dropped her way back from my back but you have not yet dropped her from your mind".

Moral of the story :

Let bygone be bygone, there is always a new sunrise to start anything anytime, do not take the burden of your past mistakes and failures on your head, forgetting the past to face the future challenge is the mantra for a successful beginning.

Perceiving others as it is, is not an easy task and perceiving yourself is rather a challenging task. Let us see how perception about others and self plays a critical role in our life with the help of some interesting concepts :

You Be You (U B U)

When I joined an MNC, I came across this concept of U B U (You Be You), it was really nice to understand your personality and be strong on that, of course bringing positive changes should always be welcomed but believing in your personality was also an important aspect they wanted to ponder on. When I went deep into the details, I understood that you are picked up because you are like you and there is no need for them to change your personality, they respect your individuality and qualities, they have accepted you with all your habits, skills and capabilities as a package and there is no logic in changing someone who is capable to enter into the system as it is. I came to know that the selection rate in that MNC was quite low and almost 1 out of 35 was picked up for critical managerial roles.

You can understand this concept even better if you answer the following question :

Question: Which of the Circles (circle A or circle B) given below is bigger :

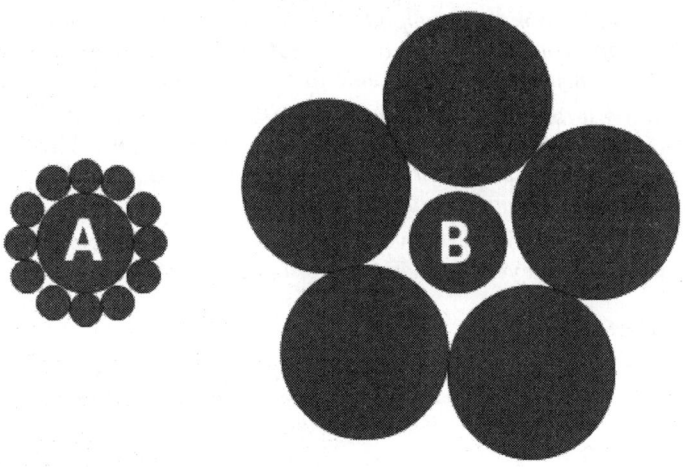

Write down your answer here :
Answer : Circle ____ is Bigger.

Now you must be inquisitive to know if your answer is right, the right answer is : Both the circles are of same size.

Although circle A *looks* bigger as it is surrounded by smaller circles and vice versa, circle B *looks* smaller as it is surrounded by bigger circles. Circle A or B (which is same size) reflects your personality. You perceive it to be smarter if you are surrounded with the people those who are not as smart as you are and you start thinking very high of you, this situation can create **Superiority Complex** and in other situation (circle B) your personality seems smaller if you are surrounded by people who are smarter than you, you start suffering with **Inferiority Complex** in this situation.

Suffering with any of the above mentioned complexes is bad, the achievement is to understand yourself fully and making a balance with your personality .

To explain this phenomenon in detail, let us see an example, just imagine you work as a manager in a firm and make Rs. 50,000/month, someday you join all your cousins in a marriage party and come to know that one of them is getting Rs. 15,000/ month, someone is getting 20,000/month and some Rs. 10,000/

Attitude Decides Altitudes

month. What feeling you will have for yourself, you will start thinking quite high about yourself and you will start boasting about your success (you may suffer with Superiority Complex here).

After a few days, you join another family function, and this time meet some cousins from other side of your family, one of your cousins is getting 2 Lakhs/month, other one gets 1.5 Lakhs/month and another one making about 2.5 Lakhs/month. What will be your feeling? Will you feel comfortable sharing that you only make Rs. 50,000/month, you may suffer with inferiority complex this time and may feel uncomfortable in their company when they talk about their international experiences and official challenges and how they manage that.

Sometimes the life is absolutely straight and simple but some incidents make it complicated, the following figure can explain this phenomenon better:

Are the horizontal lines parallel or do they slope?

Answer the question given underneath the above lines and write it down here :

The lines are _____.

The right answer to above question is – Lines are parallel, although they look slope because of the boxes in between. Now these lines denominate life, which is parallel to joy and success but sometimes seem slope because of some incidents which have taken place in our life. These incidents can be positive and negative as well, positive incidents give us the feeling of a better life than others and bad incidents sometimes make us feel as if our life is very troublesome, whenever this situation comes always chant the following phrase :

I cried for the shoes until I saw a man with no feet.
On a lighter side let us see the attitude of a baby mosquito :
A baby mosquito came back after its 1st flight. His dad asked him – "how do you feel?"
He replied, "it was wonderful, everyone was clapping for me." That's attitude.

Sometimes you must have observed that some people have got very high expectations from their wards / subordinates and to fulfill those expectations one has to work very hard and consistently, which may increase the efficiency of the individual in short run but it may be harmful in long run because of excessive pressure.

If you have a challenge in your life, your worries become very small and your pain vanishes, you concentrate on your challenges and forget other smaller issues, this is what we call as the Shark (the challenge) of our life, you will understand the concept of Shark after reading the following story.

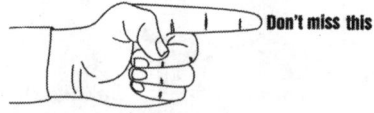 Don't miss this

The Shark in the Tank!!!

The Japanese love fresh fish. However, the waters close to Japan have not held many fish for decades. So to feed the Japanese population, fishing boats got bigger and went farther than ever. The farther the fishermen went, the longer it took to bring in the fish.

If the return trip took more than a few days, the fishes were not fresh. The Japanese did not like the taste. To solve this problem, fishing companies installed freezers on their boats. They would catch the fish and freeze them at sea. Freezers allowed the boats to go farther and stay longer.

However, the Japanese could taste the difference between fresh and frozen and they did not like frozen fish. The frozen fish brought a lower price. So fishing companies installed fish tanks. They would catch the fish and stuff them in the tanks, fin to fin. After a little thrashing around, the fish stopped moving. They were tired and dull, but alive.

Unfortunately, the Japanese could still taste the difference. Because the fish did not move for days, they lost their fresh taste. The Japanese preferred the lively taste of fresh fish and not the stale one. So how did Japanese fishing companies solve this problem? How did they get fresh-tasting fish to Japan? If you were consulting the fish industry, what would you recommend?

The problem to solve was how do fish stay fresh?

To keep the fish tasting fresh, the Japanese fishing companies still put the fishes in the tanks. But now they add a small shark to each tank. The shark eats a few fishes, but most of the fishes arrive in a very lively state because now they are challenged.

Do you have any shark in your life to keep you challenged?
I am sure you will salute the attitude and spirit of the army office if you read the following lines :
Soldier (shouting) : Sir we are surrounded by enemy from all sides.
Officer : Very Good, it means we can attack in any direction.

How the perception plays different roles for different people can be understood by the following example.

My Great Spouse

This is an example of different perceptions of a couple – Sheetal and Pankaj. Pankaj is a businessman and makes good money working hard the whole day and his wife Sheetal is a housewife always ready to spend what Pankaj makes. Let us see what happened when they went out one day for a picnic.

It was a fresh and beautiful Sunday and the sun was shining bright. Sheetal and Pankaj with their daughter Shipika and son Vidit planned to go for a picnic and en-route decided to visit a temple.

They reached the temple to worship for a bright future for their two little sweet children. While they were coming out some beggars approached them for alms and immediately Pankaj wiped out a Rs. 100 note and gave it to one of them.

Role of Perception

Situation : 1

Sheetal who observed all this got really happy and though that her husband is so nice and kind towards the poor and destitutes and helps them with open hands. She was happy that she got married to such a man who is so bothered about others too, she thought if Pankaj is so kind to the beggars, how highly concerned he will be for her and for their children. She was happy that Pankaj has gained many blessings for their children from that beggar for which she praised Pankaj and they happily moved for picnic with a very good mood.

Situation : 2

Sheetal felt very bad when she observed Pankaj throwing away his hard earned money like this. She was shocked to see that Pankaj is so low in EQ that even beggars can blackmail him emotionally. She immediately countered Pankaj and asked the logic of giving Rs.100 to the beggar. She started thinking even if they distribute all their wealth they will not be able to satisfy 10% of the beggars. She told Pankaj that in this age of high prices how difficult it is for her to manage the whole house for a month and budgeted spending is always more than the income. There she is managing somehow with household expenses, children demands, school fees, club charges, transportation,etc., and here her husband is throwing money like this which is a sheer wastage.

Situation : 3

When they came out of Temple after worshiping, Sheetal gave a Rs. 50/- to a beggar (Please note this time Sheetal has given the money). Pankaj observed this and felt very happy about the human values his wife is having and praised that how nicely she manages her home and helps poor people without disturbing the budget. Pankaj thought that the reward of her wife being so kind would definitely benefit him and their children in future and the God will be very kind on their family.

Situation : 4

As soon as Sheetal gave Rs. 50/- to a beggar, Pankaj got a shock. In this monthly income he only knows how he is managing, he has to cut a lot of expenses which are required for him keeping in mind his income. Sheetal is wasting and throwing hard earned money like this. He got so annoyed that he asked Sheetal not to do it in the future and rather save this money for the education of their children or for the rainy days.

Have you observed the role of perception in all four situations, in the first two situations, when Pankaj has given the alms, Sheetal can take it both positively and negatively and the same is the case in the last two situations, where Sheetal is giving alms and Pankaj can take it positively or negatively.

Like personal life, Perception plays a very critical role in corporate world also, few things which are highly appreciated by one type of bosses may be taken very negatively by other type of bosses. I can quote many examples but here I will quote only one example for which I am not having any answer as yet, few years back I made a Structured Interview Form so that similar type of questions can be asked from all candidates coming for interview so that we can compare their answers, when I presented it to my boss, he got really annoyed and asked me if I believe in his interviewing techniques or not, he refused to accept the structured interview process and I have to listen a lot for this action.

Few years back, when I joined an American MNC and we started recruiting other employees, my boss scolded me for not making a structured interview form. I told him about my previous experience about the structured interview form. After listening to me my current boss criticised my previous boss to be over confident and gave me a lecture on how the best recruitments can be done only with structured interview (actually I was heading HR and I should have told him all this, but...Boss is always right).

To Win a *War*, you need to Lose some *Battles*.

It means for **long-term success you need to sometimes lose in short-term.** Some theories in life are suitable for short run only and some are fruitful for long run. Some may be good in short run initially but may turn the other way round and vice versa. Some may be pinching or bad in the beginning (i.e. in short run) and may turn to be absolutely rewarding in the long run. The attitude of short run can sometimes spoil the success of long run. This can be understood with the help of the following story of a man called Bahadur :

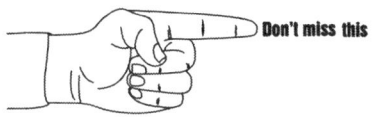

Bahadur's Attitude

There was a watchman in Bengal, his name was Bahadur (meaning 'brave') and as per the name he was very brave. One night when he was on duty some thieves entered the complex where he was doing his duty and due to his alertness and bravery all the thieves were caught. The company where he was working was very happy and sent him to Goa for a complimentary trip with full lodging and boarding facilities.

He was happy to be in Goa. One day when he was roaming on the beach it went dark and while returning he kicked a bottle lying on the beach and it collided with a rock and broke. To Bahadur's shock, a genie came out of the bottle and said – "Thank You for freeing me from the bottle. I was captured in it for many years. I am very happy and want to grant you 4 wishes. Ask whatever you want to ask as I need to go to my world."

Bahadur got shocked and started shivering, he requested the genie to vanish without even granting a wish as he was terrified with his huge and muscular body. But the genie kept insisting him for four wishes.

Bahadur with great shyness told the Genie that he will be very happy and rather thankful if Genie constructs a house on the beach.

The Genie swished in a second and with magic a huge beautiful bungalow just appeared on the beach from nowhere. The Genie said – "Here is your first wish, ask for the other three"

Bahadur was very happy but surprised and got some confidence and believe in Genie, he was continuously looking towards the big bungalow and was very happy, he gathered some courage and told Genie that he will very happy if a car can also be provided.

> *A positive attitude is like a magic wand, you can almost have anything in a swish...*

In a swish the Genie got a 7 Series BMW in front of the bungalow and told Bahadur that here is the Car, what else, you have got 2 more wishes, ask me anything and you will get it today.

Bahadur was very happy and quite confident and now it was the time to ask for his 3rd wish. Bahadur gathered the courage and explained Jinni that a Bungalow and Car is useless without the sweet lady owner of these.

Genie understood, praised Bahadur for his thoughtfulness and in a swish again he managed to get a very beautiful girl sitting in the car, Genie asked Bahadur for the last wish so that he can vanish.

Bahadur, who was very excited by now started thanking Jinni again and again.

Genie was getting restless with the time he was spending, he asked Bahadur to ask for the last wish quickly so that he can vanish, when he pressed Bahadur to ask for last wish.

Bahadur said : "Make me the Watchman of this House Please."

Ha Ha Ha... this is attitude, even if you are getting everything in life, you may lose everything with your poor attitude, in this joke the attitude of a watchman remained of a watchman only and he could not adjust his attitude, neither he could become the owner of the house and car nor could marry that beautiful girl.

Have you checked what is your attitude, are you sure it is positive and have you been benefitted with it, can you further improve it.

It is better to sacrifice your Ego for your Love rather than sacrificing your Love for your Ego.

Someone asked : Why have we so many temples if God is everywhere.

Answer : Just like Fans, even if Air is everywhere you need a fan to feel it.

Your Value is not because of the People who praise you in your presence, your value is people praising you in your absence.

Glass Half Full or Half Empty

The Age old riddle of attitude is redefined now (I do not have a Patent or Copy write on this and that is why you can use it freely)...

Gone are the days when people claiming that it is half empty were considered to be negative thinkers, now a days even people claiming that it is Half Full are also known as only thinkers (and not necessarily as positive thinkers)

The right answer is : it is Full, half with water and half with air.

Rather I will say even if there is no water in the glass, still it is full (of course- full with air)

Let us see another amazing example of different perspectives of life :

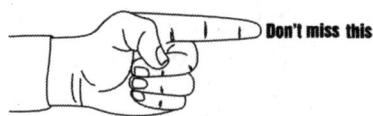

Why Me ???

Whenever anything goes wrong, we ask from God – Why me, although when something is going great, we just keep quite; let us share a story of Legendary Wimbledon player and the winner of many grand slams – Arthur Ashe and let us see what we can learn from it :

Arthur Ashe was infected with blood he got during a heart surgery in 1983. Letters poured in from all over the world, as he was dying of AIDS. One letter asked, 'Why has GOD chosen you for such a bad disease'?

To this, Arthur Ashe replied:

'The world over -- 50 million children start playing tennis, 5 million learn to play tennis, 500,000 learn professional tennis, 50,000 come to the circuit, 5000 reach the Grand Slam, 50 reach Wimbledon , 4 to semifinal, 2 to the finals.

'When I was holding the Wimbledon Cup I never asked GOD 'Why me?'

And today in pain I should not be asking GOD 'Why me?'.....

This is what is Positive Attitude, even if you are suffering, the positive thinking will make it less painful, even if you are failing, you can take a turn with positive thinking to be a winner but for that you need to start believing and bringing changes in your thought process.

If you do not bring a positive change in your thought process, you will be like the Elephant which was ties with a very thin chain and was not knowing or believing that it can easily break it, we call it Elephant Mindset :

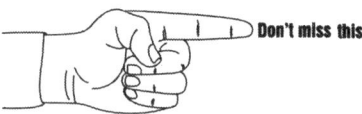 Don't miss this

Elephant Mindset!!

One of my friends went to southern India and observed a very interesting fact when he visited an elephant century, he observed that the baby elephants were tied up with thick and strong iron chains and the big elephants were tied with very thin and weak chains.

He was surprised and asked about the reason from 'Mahavat' (elephant caretaker).

The 'Mahavat' explained : we tie baby elephant with a strong and thick iron chain because it will try its level best to break it open and run away to play with other baby elephants, it tries and tries hard, pull it, jerk it and tries every trick to break it with its trunk.

After some days the baby elephant understands that it cannot break the chain and then it stops trying, when it grows up and become a big strong elephant, we just tie it with a thin and weak chain but now it never tries to break it open as its believe is stronger that it cannot break it, he forgets that now he is big and strong enough to break it but its believe work stronger and he does not even try to break it.

Moral of the Story:
1) *If you could not do something sometimes back, doesn't mean you will never be able to do that.*
2) *If you believe in your strengths, you can break the chains stopping you to achieve your goals.*
3) *Break all believes, which are hindrances in your path to success.*
4) *Do not lose heart by mere presence of difficulties, analyse them, you can solve these with your determination and strength.*

On the Lighter Side, let us enjoy the following management lesson...

Management Lesson
A turkey was chatting with a bull. "I would love to be able to get to the top of that tree, sighed the turkey, but I haven't got the energy. Well, why don›t you nibble on some of my droppings? replied the bull.
They're packed with nutrients.
The turkey pecked at a lump of dung and found that it actually gave him enough strength to reach the first branch of the tree.
The next day, after eating some more dung, he reached the second branch. Finally after a fortnight, there he was proudly perched at the top of the tree.
Soon he was promptly spotted by a farmer, who shot the turkey out of the tree.

Learnings from Lesson:
Bullshit might get you to the top, but it won't keep you there.

Regular naps prevent old age, especially if you take them while driving.

3

SKILLED ABILITIES

(The Magic Starts from Here...)

Consistent people can reach somewhere, non-consistent are known as 'some were'

Skilled Abilities

We all need some skills and abilities to face the challenges of life to be successful, but before we discuss about the skilled abilities, I want to share that in some cases we do not need any ability to perform some regular tasks. Sometimes we make our life unnecessarily difficult by making a simple hurdle a big problem.

I am sure it can sound silly to some of you that if there is no problem, how can some people treat it as a problem. Is it because of their nature. They unnecessarily waste time and energy in solving 'no problems.' Let me explain this phenomenon with the help of a story :

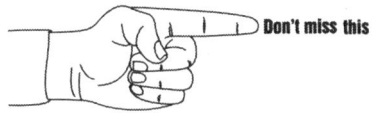
Don't miss this

The Great Magician

Once upon a time there was a great magician in the West and his ability was to open all types of locks in seconds. He challenged people to lock him, handcuff him, chain him, put him in coffins with many locks on it and throw him in the sea and he came out in minutes opening all locks and breaking all chains.

He travelled all over the world challenging many people. Every time he would come out in minutes opening all locks.

He finally reached India and threw the same challenge.

Indians took the challenge and planned to defeat him. On the day of the challenge they took him to a house, left him there and came out. Now it was magician's turn to come out as soon as possible.

People outside the house waited for hours but the magician could not come out. When they thought that the magician has lost the challenge, he came out of the house completely drenched in sweat. He was dead tired and could not walk. He somehow managed to talk and told the audience that

he had lost this challenge, he said – *"I am a specialist in opening the locks and I kept on looking and searching for locks but there was no lock on the door, I tried to search the lock everywhere on the doors, so that I can show my mastery, my blood pressure kept on shooting, my heart beat and pulse was going high as I was thinking that today I am going to lose my earned respect and fame, but was not able to locate the locks. After many hours when I got exhausted and accepted my defeat, I fell on the door and it opened outside because.... there was no lock".*

Moral of the Story :
Sometimes in our life there is no problem, there is no challenge but we are not able to see this. We take simple riddles as challenges and wastes our time and energy on some issues which are not even required to be given attention, we should invest our energy in bigger challenges rather than petty issues, a positive outlook in life will sharpen our 'Skills and Abilities' to be successful.

First you need to believe that you have got the desired skills to be successful and you need to sharpen them more to reach on a point from where you can use them as a weapon to fight your battle. You need to keep on inculcating the habits (the details of some productive habits are given in the chapter of Habits) of sharpening these skills to abilities as you need to sow the seeds to get the expected fruits and unexpected success.

The following paragraph regarding the Chinese bamboo will clarify this point :

CHINESE BAMBOO

We should be like the farmer who grows Chinese bamboo. After the bamboo is planted, only a tiny shoot is visible and the gardener must tend and nurture the bamboo for four years while the shoot remains the size of a thumb. For those first four years all the growth takes place underground, unseen, in the plant's root system.

Finally, in the fifth year, the gardener's perseverance is rewarded as the bamboo grows 80 feet in a year !!!

Similarly, when you will start investing in sowing the seeds of good habits and sharpening your skills to abilities to be successful. You need to be a little patient (not for years like the Chinese farmer but for few months) before you get to see some amazing results.

ABILITIES

You just need to sharpen your skills into abilities to be successful

Abilities can be divided into two categories – **functional abilities** and **behavioural abilities.** To be successful both these types of abilities are required in right proportion. Where functional abilities help you in solving functional challenges, the behavioural abilities help you in sharpening your personality to face the behavioural challenges by managing people around you. Although this chapter is dedicated to functional abilities, the following chapters are based on behavioural ability. Although no one can have these abilities in a day and you need constant practice to inculcate the habit of understanding and utilising these abilities for the best results.

This chapter will have stories in place of any long theories and descriptions to communicate the real message in a different but effective manner, let us start with functional abilities.

The following are some **functional abilities,** you need to sharpen to succeed in Life :

Ability 1 : Strong Memory

Who in the whole world will not like to have a strong memory. We think (just think only) that some people are blessed with a good memory, I can challenge and bet that we all can have a strong memory if we show some interest in learning some basic techniques. While taking orientation for MBA Students, I have shown the skills of memory by remembering a list of 30 different items made by them randomly in a minute and then narrating the whole list from 1 to 30 and in reverse order from 30 to 1 without any mistake. I let them call the number and I tell them what was the item on that particular number or reverse- I let them take the name of the item and I tell them it was on which number in that list. They were amazed to see how someone can remember a list made by them randomly and how it is possible for him to even know the exact number of the item or item on the exact number and that too in just one minute.

Let me tell you, this is very easy, a bit of homework is required from your side and two techniques of memory known as 'Association or Link' and 'Hook' technique will help you out in memorising a list of items in perfect order, numbered lists, cell phone numbers, etc. Important data and information, faces, names and many more things which generally people think are very difficult to remember can be easily memorised with the help of these techniques.

There is another technique known as **Mnemonics**, which we will see in this chapter. Also we will get to know how we can use different mnemonics to remember different things, which are very difficult to remember otherwise.

Association or Link Technique of Memory – You can associate what you need to remember with a pre remembered memory or some object and as soon as you think about the subject the picture you have saved with the help of association will come up to help you out.

Example 1 : Remembering the date of purchase of our first scooter

I asked my father when we purchased our first scooter and in a second he told me 30th January 1972. I was amazed to listen to the exact date and just inquired how he can remember the exact date and year, he happily told me that it was my first birthday, how someone can forget his first son's birthday and the purchase of scooter was associated or linked to that permanent soothing incident.

Then I asked him when we purchased our first car, he could not give me any exact date except an idea like in mid of 1993, now this date was not exact as there is no association or link with the date.

Example 2 : Remembering the passport number

If I ask you to remember my passport number which is 15081947, you may not remember it but if I put the number in the order of 15 08 1947 and tell you that this was the date when we got freedom, you can never forget my passport number.

Skilled Abilities

What we need to start learning is the association and link technique which is very easy.

Example 3 : Remembering the days in each month of the year

Now remembering that January has got 31 days, February 28/29 days, March 31 and April 30 can be a tedious exercise and it is difficult to answer all of a sudden if someone asked you how many days August has? You are confused whether to say 30 or 31. Let me help you out in remembering this with your fist knuckles.

How to remember number of days in a month

Make your fist, see towards your knuckles, there are mountain peaks (of knuckles) and ditches (between the knuckles). Give 31 to peaks and 30 to ditches, this way the first knuckle (peak) is January and the ditch between the first and second knuckle is February, the second knuckle peak is March and the ditch between the second and third knuckle is April, just in the same manner as shown in the above picture.

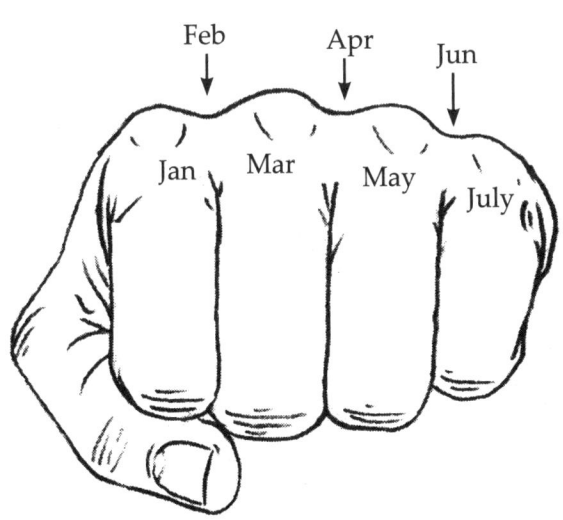

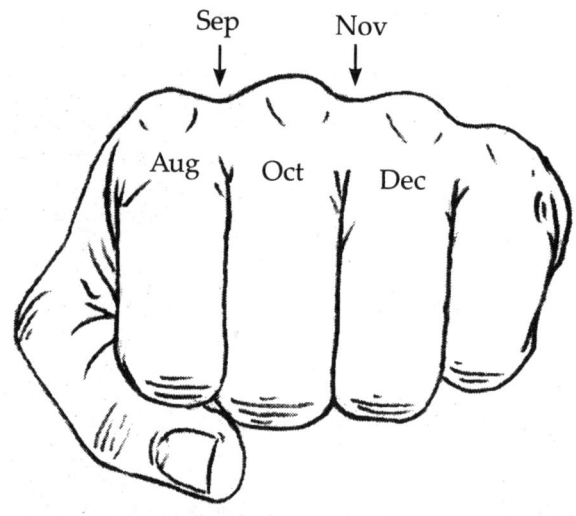

Now it is very simple for you to remember, the mountain (knuckle) is 31 days and the ditch (the space between the two knuckles) is 30 days (just with one exception of February, which is 29 days in a leap year and 28 in others).

Similarly when you count upto July then August will again come from first knuckle (peak) and similarly this goes on.

Just practise and note that how easy it is for you to remember the days of the months.

Example 4 : *Remembering the colours of rainbow in right order :*

Here the Mnemonics is simple and that is : VIBGYOR (for seven colours of Rainbow - V=violet, I = indigo, B=blue, G=green, Y=yellow, O=orange and R=red. How simple it is.

Example 5 : *Remembering trigonometry values*

Sin Theta is P/H
Cos Theta is B/H
Tan Theta is P/B
Cot Theta is B/P

Sec Theta is H/B
Cosec Theta is H/P
that is why sin theta is 1/cosec and cosec is 1/Sin
that is why cos theta is 1/sec and Sec is 1/cos
that is why Tan theta is 1/cot and cot is 1/tan

now remembering above can be a challenge for a normal person but if you use mnemonics here, you can never forget it, let us remember a single interesting line :

After looking towards Trigonometry – *'Pandit Badri Prashad Hari Hari Bole'*

Let us write the above statement in a format of 3 words in table like :

Pundit **(P)**	Badri **(B)**	Prashad **(P)**
Hari **(H)**	Hari **(H)**	Bole **(B)**

Now we have got a pattern of putting Thetas in this table in the direction of aeros:.

Sin	Cos	Tan
P	B	P
H	H	B
Cosec	Sec	Cot

Now see just looking at the table once you can easily recall any of the thetas. Go to where we discussed thetas and see how easy it is for you to remember trigonometric thetas.

(For more insights into memory techniques, you can refer to Harry Lorayne. He is amazing in these techniques).

Drifting away a bit, let us enjoy a very interesting case to see how different people make use of their abilities, this is an interesting paradox :

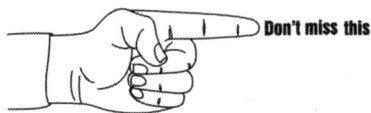

The Lawyer's Dilemma

Many years ago, a law teacher came across a student who was willing to learn but was unable to pay the fees. The student struck a deal saying, "I will pay your fee the day I win my first case in the court". The teacher agreed and proceeded with the law course. When the course finished and the teacher started pestering the student to pay up the fee, the student reminded him of the deal and pushed days. Fed  up with this, the teacher decided to sue the student in the court of law and both of them decided to argue for themselves.

The teacher put forward his argument saying: "If I win this case, as per the court of law, the student has to pay me as the case is about his non-payment of dues. And if I lose the case, student will still pay me because he would have won his first case. So either ways I will get the money".

Equally brilliant, the student with equal abilities argued back saying: "If I win the case, as per the court of law, I don't have to pay anything to the teacher as the case is about my non-payment of dues. And if I lose the case, I don't have to pay him because I haven't won my first case yet. So either way, I am not going to pay the teacher anything".

Ability 2 : Consistency and Perseverance

People feel motivated suddenly (most of the times this is external motivation, details are covered in the chapter of motivation) and they will start doing something but may stop in between, sometimes even on slightest of the problem. They feel frustrated, bored and loss of interest or energy in the work they picked up, sometimes they even do not believe in their decisions and keep on changing their decisions to be successful overnight, which may not be possible.

The following very important story will clarify the value and importance of consistency and perseverance, which we all should have as a strong ability to proceed further.

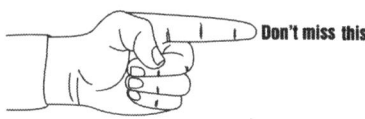

The Story of Two Farmers

There was a saint who was on a tour to rural India with his pupils. They pledged to 'take' pleasure by 'giving' and visited many states and villages to help people in whatever manner they could.

Where they taught many things, they also learnt many lessons, one such learning was very unexpected when they were crossing one of the villages. They observed a very strange site – they saw a huge field divided by a fence in between having one side of the field completely green, full of crops, big green fruitful trees with birds chirping on the branches and the owner - the farmer was sitting on a cot playing with his kids. They were happy and were joking, dancing and enjoying, their mother was cooking something energetically on the earthen stove on the side of the field and was looking quite happy. This site was of a very happy family.

But surprisingly on the other side of the fence of the same field, there was nothing. It looked like a barren land which was digged all over.

There were big and small pits, no crops, no trees, no greenery at all and the sad family of the owner (another farmer) was sitting in a corner hut, just doing nothing, kids were hungry and crying, having nothing to eat. There was nothing on the cold stove, no joy, no life, nothing.

All the pupils of the saint were shocked and surprised to see all this for the first time in their life. How a huge big field can be lush green on one side of the fence and completely barren on the other side. They looked at the Saint with the question mark in their eyes, the Saint could have replied easily but advised the pupils to get the answer themselves(hold for a while and try to guess the reason yourself). The pupils, bound with their oath of helping the world, first approached the poor farmer on the barren portion of the field - who was sad, to share his sorrows and asked him – "How did this happen." The farmer told them that he came to know well in advance that monsoon will not come this year, so he decided to dig a well in the field. He identified a place where he thought the water will come out and started digging, 5 meters, 10 meters, nothing happened. He lost hope soon and identified another place to dig the well. He again got disheartened and changed the place, again started digging but upto 30 meters nothing happened, he tried few more times half-heartedly and got no water, rather the whole field was dug with no result. He started cursing the fate, got disheartened and left trying.

Pupils were emotionally sympathetic to him and thought what could be done to help him. Before helping him they thought of checking with the other farmer, who was on the other side of the fence, happy in his green field with flourishing crops and fruits. They wanted to know the reason of his prosperity and so approached the happy farmer and asked the same question, "How did this happen"?

The happy farmer replied that he came to know in advance that monsoon will not come this year and therefore decided to dig a well in the field. He identified a place where he thought the water will come out and started digging, 5 meters, 10 meters, nothing happened. But he did not lose hope, believed in his decisions and abilities and kept on digging. He continued digging 15 meters, 20 meters, nothing happened, finally he dug more than 50 meters. That is when the water came out, clear, sweet and cold water, water full of life, full of energy and full of blessings. The farmer irrigated his field with this water and as a result the field was lush green.

What have you learnt, what is the lesson, it is consistency, perseverance and belief in yourself, taking and trusting your decisions, that is what the happy farmer did.

Skilled Abilities 59

How many times, we just blame our luck or fate and how many times do we try. Do we take our own decisions and believe in ourselves? Do we have the energy to be consistent in our efforts? Do we accept the problems of life as a challenge? In place of asking the God - "Why Me', let us start asking the God - 'Try Me', and see the amazing results.

Ability 3 : Facing the Challenges and Adverse Situations

Life will not go smooth, were you will win some battles, you will lose some also, the next ability is the courage and power of facing challenges and adverse situations, a lot of people lose hope early and let it happen to them. The winners face the challenges and take the problems head on. They come up with solutions and the troubles make them even stronger.

To understand this ability, let us see how a Donkey, who fell in a well faced the challenge of his life.

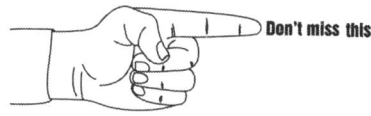 Don't miss this

Donkey in the Well

One day a farmer's donkey fell down into a well. The animal cried piteously for hours as the farmer tried to figure out what to do. Finally, the farmer decided the animal was old, and the well needed to be covered up anyway and it is just not worth it to retrieve the donkey.

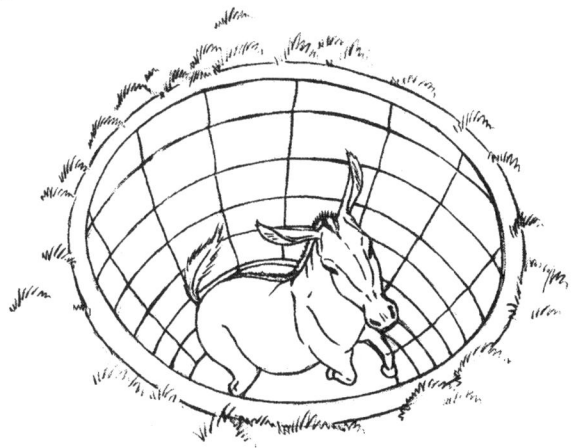

He invited all his neighbours to come over and help him. They all grabbed a shovel and began to shovel dirt into the well to fill it up to the top. At first, the donkey realized what was happening and cried horribly. Then, to everyone's amazement he quieted down.

A few shovel loads later, the farmer finally looked down the well. He was astonished at what he saw, the donkey was doing something amazing, with each shovel of dirt that hit Donkey's back, the Donkey would shake it off and take a step up.

As the farmer's neighbours continued to shovel dirt on top of the animal, he would shake it off and take a step up.

Pretty soon, everyone was amazed as the donkey stepped up over the edge of the well and happily trotted off!

Moral of the Story :

Life may shovel dirt on you, all kinds of dirt. The trick to get out of the problem is to shake it off and take a step up. Each of our troubles is a stepping stone. We can get out of the deepest wells just by not stopping, never giving up! Shake it off and take a step up.

Ability 4 : Prioritisation of Tasks and Actions

Your life is how you prioritise it and how you give importance to essential tasks. The following story of a professor, who taught the same to his students, will help you out in learning this ability.

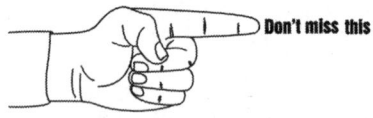 Don't miss this

Empty Jar and Two Cups of Coffee

A professor - Hem Prakash Joshi stood before his philosophy class and had some items in front of him. When the class began, wordlessly, he picked up a very large and empty jar and proceeded to fill it with golf balls. He then asked the students, if the jar was full. They agreed that it was.

The professor then picked up a box of pebbles and poured them into the jar. He shook the jar lightly. The pebbles rolled into the open areas between the golf balls. He then asked the students again if the jar was full...

Skilled Abilities

They agreed it was. The professor next picked up a box of sand and poured it into the jar. Of course, the sand filled up everything else.

He asked once more if the jar was full. The students responded with a unanimous 'yes.' The professor then produced two cups of coffee from under the table and poured the entire contents into the jar, effectively filling the empty space between the sand. The students laughed.

'Now,' said the professor, as the laughter subsided,' I want you to recognize that this jar represents your life.

The golf balls are the important things - God, spouse, children, health, friends, and your passions and hobbies. If everything else was lost and only they remained, your life would still be full.

The pebbles are the other things that matter like your job, house and car, etc. The sand is everything else - the small stuff.

'If you put the sand into the jar first,' he continued, "there is no room for the pebbles or the golf balls." The same goes for life. If you spend all your time and energy on the small stuff, you will never have room for the things that are important to you.

So, pay attention to the things that are critical to your happiness. Spend time with your spouse. Play with your children. Take time to get medical checkups. Take your partner out to dinner.

There will always be time to clean the house and fix the disposal. 'Take care of the golf balls' first - The things that really matter. Set your priorities. The rest is just sand.'

One of the students raised her hand and inquired what the coffee represented. The professor smiled. 'I'm glad you asked'. It just goes to show you that no matter how full your life may seem, there's always room for a cup of coffee with a friend.' !!!

Ability 5 : Believing in Yourself

How can you compare yourself with others? What they will have, you may not? What you are blessed with, others may not even dream of? Just concentrate on your abilities to believe in yourself. When I tried to be the first jogger in the morning and woke up quite early, I found someone running already in the park there should not be a rat race as the ability of believing in yourself will help you out in finding your path of success.

The following story of poor farmer Hasan will help you out in learning how to start believing in your abilities and start working towards success.

King the Beggar

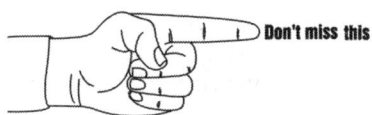 **Don't miss this**

There was poor farmer Hasan in a village, who was tense because of the draught that year which shook all farmers and compelled them to starve. Hasan decided to have a well in his field so that he need not to be dependent on the rain every year, but there was a big problem of money. The well digging required a big work force and many tools, he needed a lot of money and he had no money.

Hasan was tense about how to arrange money and from where. Who is so rich to lend some money and after thinking a lot, decided to explain his condition to his kind King to get some money from him, who was famous for his charity.

Skilled Abilities

Hasan left his village for the King's Palace in the Capital City. After reaching the palace he requested the gatekeeper and explained that he has come all the way from a far off village to see the king for some help.

The gatekeeper attended him well and asked him to wait for some time as the king was offering evening prayers. Hasan was allowed only upto the prayer room but was instructed not to disturb the king until the prayers were over. Hasan sat outside the prayer room, which had a beautiful cloth curtain which was swinging in the air.

It was getting darker and now Hasan wanted to meet the king as early as possible so that he could start back for his village soon. His patience was getting over and he decided to enter the prayer room to meet the king.

Although it was a big decision, but he entered the prayer room and observed the king sitting on his knees with open arms towards the sky. The King was asking for health, wealth and prosperity from the God. Hasan was shocked, he thought that the king had everything he needed in the world and still he is asking for everything from God. Hasan thought for a while and reached on a conclusion that if God had the power to give anything to anyone even to the Kings then why to ask from King, why can't he get everything straight from God.

Hasan quickly turned back and came out of the palace and when the gatekeeper asked him about his meeting with king, he said, "I could not meet the king but I got the solution of my problem. I will ask the God to give me the power to solve my problems so that I need not to beg anything from anybody even if the other person is a King."

Hasan returned to his village and called all villagers to tell them about the incident. He told them how the King was asking for everything from God. He asked all the villagers to ask from God to give them power and courage to solve their problems and take their own decisions. Today all of them learnt a very important lesson of their life to believe in themselves and to believe in their abilities rather than being dependent on others.

They all decided to help each other in digging the wells and picked up the shovels to start the work, they believed in themselves and needed just the courage to dig some wells for them.

When they all joined hands, they first dug a well for Hasan, as soon as the fresh, cold water came up, they felt motivated to dig some more for others in that village for helping each other and turned the barren land into the most productive one.

This is what happens when we believe in ourselves and help each other.

It is not only the question of believing in your physical abilities, you need to believe in your mental abilities as well, even if you are not physically strong enough but if you sharpen the ability of accepting the challenges, you will be able to overcome the riddles with amazing colours, this point can be learnt better with the following story, where a small sparrow faced the challenge and defeated the mighty python with her mental ability

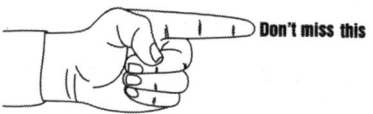

Don't miss this

Intelligent Sparrow

There was sparrow living on a tree for many years. The tree was a permanent house for her as she laid her eggs every year on that tree only, the chickens came out, she fed them and they flew off to new destinations on new journey with new challenges. Her life was comfortable upto the time a python came and occupied the stem hole of the tree, python was very lazy and never wanted to go out in search of food, he always wished that someone could bring food for him in his house only.

Once, when the sparrow laid the eggs and was away in search of food, the python ate her eggs. When she returned, she got shocked and broken, she cried and moaned over the happening and quickly

Skilled Abilities 65

understood who has done that, she was restless and wanted to teach a lesson to the python but she felt helpless, how she can fight and confront such a huge python.

Sometimes we are in the same situation, we also think helplessly how to fight with bigger challenges in life, we think that we are weak and cannot stand against big challenges, at this time we need to sit quietly to do some rational decision making (details are covered in the chapter of decision making) with the cool mind, the ability to believe in yourself and the power of decision making will help you out in facing the toughest challenges of your life, let us see how the little sparrow handled this challenge.

After crying and weeping for days together, she sat quietly and believed in her ability to take decisions, she used her brain power, thought and reached on a conclusion to take an action (only planning will not help you out, effective planning with flawless execution is the formula for assured success) to get rid of the huge culprit python.

With a strong plan in her mind and with a will to execute this effectively, she flew towards the river and started searching for the queen of the state, who used to come for having a bath at the nearby river but could not locate her. She again looked for her the next day but could not locate her, this went on for many days but she was not able to locate the queen.

This also happens in our lives, we do not get the desired results whenever we want, sometimes it takes its own sweet time, we need to be relaxed and concentrating in our work, the opportunities will surely come and we should be ready to grab them as and when they appear.

The same thing happened with her as well, one day the queen came to swim in the river and kept her clothes and ornaments on the river bank to enter the river with her friends, when she finished and came out to wear her clothes and ornaments, the sparrow jumped on her necklace, picked it up in her beak and flew towards the jungle, the queen shouted aloud and the bodyguards rushed towards the sparrow, the sparrow flew towards the stem hole (the house of the python), who as usually was sleeping, hoping to get the food supplied there only.

She ensured that the bodyguards chase her to the right point and in front of them only she dropped the necklace in the hole, just over the head of the sleeping python, the bodyguards reached the tree and wanted to retrieve the necklace at any cost, they searched with their spokes and spears and could see a huge python, they had to kill the python to get the necklace back and returned towards the queen.

The sparrow looked at all this from a nearby tree, she was satisfied to take her revenge from an untrustworthy neighbour, although she was not powerful enough physically but with her mental ability and belief, she was able to get rid of the mighty python.

Are we like this sparrow, do we also believe in our mental powers and abilities, do we also plan flawlessly, do we execute our plans effectively?, are the questions we need to ask ourselves.

Ability 6 : Intelligence and Smartness

The question is not how intelligent and smart you are, the question is whatever is the level, how and where do you use it, many people believe that they are very smart, it is their belief only if they do not prove and others do not recognise. Your intelligence should take you to the path of success otherwise it is of no use. Let us share an interesting story of a very intelligent and smart Goldsmith and a King, who thought he is intelligent and believed that he can make a fool of everyone, who was smart that you need to recognise after reading the story, let us enjoy the story first :

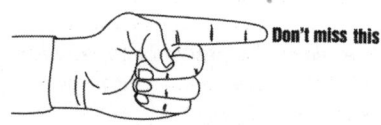
Don't miss this

Goldsmith

There was a King who always thought himself one of the smartest men on earth. He never trusted people around him and always wanted to keep an eye on them. Due to his nature he lost good friends around him and was surrounded by yes-men.

One day the king called one of his ministers and told him that he wanted to gift a Garland made of gold to his queen on her birthday, which was falling next month. He asked the minister to call a good goldsmith for it.

The Minister who was one of his yes-men, got this opportunity to impress the king and advised him not to buy any Gold Garland from any Goldsmith as he claimed that all the goldsmiths are crooks and can steel some gold in this transaction.

The King who always considered himself very smart told his Minister not to worry as he would get the goldsmith make the garland in the palace only in the presence of the guards. Pure gold was issued to him from the Palace treasury itself so that the goldsmith cannot do any hanky panky. This way the kind was sure enough that now he will be able to get a Pure Gold Garland for his queen.

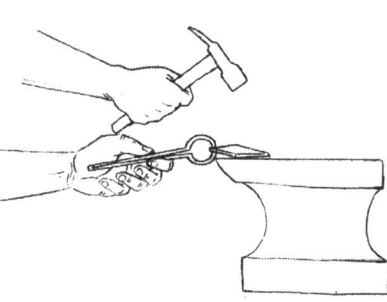

When one of the goldsmiths was called and explained the task, the goldsmith felt bad because the King did not trust him but had to agree to the task which was going to take one month.

The goldsmith reported with his tools next day and was searched properly and was told that he will be searched daily while coming in and going out to make sure that the garland made by him is of pure gold and also to ensure that no gold is stolen and the goldsmith does not take copper inside.

The goldsmith started the work and continued making it for almost one month. During this period, sometimes the minister and king himself came personally to check how he was working and checked the garland themselves.

After about a month, the goldsmith told the King that the garland was ready. The king checked the beautiful masterpiece and appreciated the goldsmith for his hard work. The king was not only happy with the craftsmanship but was also contented that he managed to get a garland made of pure gold.

The goldsmith requested the king that if he permits, he would like to wash the garland in the river water so that the shine of the garland can be enhanced. He told the king that it would glitter more if it is properly washed and rubbed in the running water of the river. The King agreed and ordered his soldiers to accompany the goldsmith.

The goldsmith surrounded with soldiers went to the river and washed the garland properly, came back to the palace and gave it to the king. The king observed that the garland was really glittering a lot and was looking so good that he announced a heavy prize for the goldsmith and praised him in front of all his ministers.

The goldsmith thanked the king, took his prize and left happily. On the queen's birthday the king gifted the garland to her with a great pride. The queen was very happy to have such a nice gift and thanked the king again and again.

The king boasted about his smartness and told the queen, how he called the goldsmith to his palace for one full month and gave him pure gold so that there was no chance of mixing. The king boasted a lot and claimed that it was not only difficult but impossible to ditch him as he is very smart and intelligent.

The queen was very sensible and mature. She immediately calculated that due to the king's behaviour the goldsmith must have felt bad and would have done something to teach the king a lesson.

She asked the king to get the garland tested with some other experienced goldsmiths to ensure that it is made of pure gold. The king smiled and accepted her offer, as he was very sure that nothing could be wrong as it is made of pure gold given by him from the palace and is manufactured in the presence of the security guards.

The king called some experienced goldsmiths and proudly asked them to check if the particular garland is made of gold. All the goldsmiths checked it carefully. They tested the garland with a special stone and with a few chemicals and told the king that the garland was made of copper only and not gold.

The King and all the ministers were shocked and surprised as the garland was made in the palace in the presence of so many guards.

The concerned goldsmith who made the garland, was called and asked about this riddle. The goldsmith laughed a lot and told the king that he did not like the attitude of the king as he thought of himself to be the smartest and wanted to teach him a lesson by giving him a garland made of copper and not gold

The king and the ministers were ashamed and felt sorry for their behaviour but they were still confused how he has done this miracle of changing pure gold with copper as he was being frisked day and night while coming in and going out from the palace.

The goldsmith now revealed the secret

Do you want to know the secret? How was it done? or can you guess?

OK, let us listen to what the Goldsmith told the King :

"When I decided to give a copper garland, I purchased a lot of copper from the market and started manufacturing the same type of garland during night time at my residence. Because in the daytime I was making the original gold

Skilled Abilities 69

garland in the palace, it was very easy for me to make the same design of the duplicate copper garland during night time at my residence. One day prior to finishing the original garland in the palace, I finished the duplicate one at my residence and during night time only went to the river, pricked a nail on the river bank wall under the water and hanged the duplicate copper garland there. Next day when I finished the original gold garland in the palace, I got the permission to wash it in the flowing river. When I reached the river and was washing the original gold garland under the water, I changed both the garlands and came out from river with the duplicate copper garland, which was of similar pattern and the same duplicate copper garland was given to the king".

The king was quite surprised over the smartness of the goldsmith, learnt a lesson and gave him a prize for his intelligent work. The gist of the story is that you need to believe in your abilities and you can teach a lesson to the people who think they are over smart.

Ability 7 : Perfection and Pride in your Work

How can you even dream of succeeding without loving your work, if you love your work, you will gain perfection and will feel proud in doing so, if we all learn this ability to love our work and start taking pride in it, there is no power on earth, which can stop us in achieving our goals.

Let us learn from the following story of a Sculptor, who achieved perfection and took pride in his work

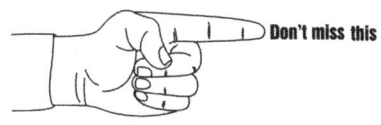 Don't miss this

Scar on Statue

A gentleman once visited a temple under construction where he saw a sculptor making an idol of God. Suddenly he noticed a similar idol lying nearby.

Surprised, he asked the sculptor, "Do you need two statues of the same idol?" "No," said the sculptor without looking up, "We need only one, but the first one got damaged at the last stage."

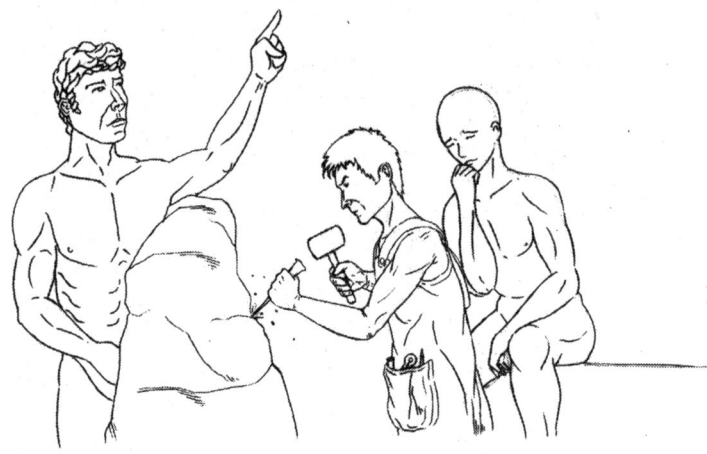

The gentleman examined the idol and found no apparent damage. "Where is the damage?" he asked. "There is a scratch on the nose of the idol." said the sculptor, still busy with his work.

"Where are you going to install the idol?" The sculptor replied that it would be installed on a pillar twenty feet high. "If the idol is that far, who is going to know that there is a scratch on the nose?" the gentleman asked.

The sculptor stopped his work, looked up at the gentleman, smiled and said, "I know it and God knows it!"

> The desire to excel should be exclusive of the fact whether someone appreciates it or not. "Excellence" is a drive from inside, not outside. Excel at a task today - not necessarily for someone else to notice but for your own satisfaction ! !

Ability 8 : Be on your Own and Don't be a Puppet in the Hands of Others

You be You and be on your own, do not be a puppet in the hands of others, plan your path yourself, execute with full confidence, make use of your abilities and capabilities and do not let others control you at all.

I have seen in the corporate world, the so called big bosses are also sometimes the puppets of bigger bosses, if you accept

Skilled Abilities 71

this situation, you will be lost in your eyes, you will not know who you are if you keep on following whatever is told. You should never forget that God has given you a backbone and a proud brain on it to use, just dancing on the tones of others will make you a puppet and mind it puppets can't be successful and the credit will go to the master and not to the puppet.

The following story of a small boy who went to a fare with his father, will help you in understanding this ability.

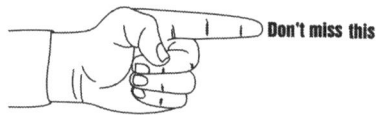

Puppet and The Innocent Child

There was an innocent child – Shrey, who was rewarded by his Father for obtaining many medals in Swimming, his father took him to Delhi Haat ('haat' is a market), where he enjoyed a lot. while coming back he insisted for a Puppet as he liked the puppet show very much and wanted to buy one.

His father took him to the puppet seller and Shrey picked up a puppet and placed it on the ground so that it can dance, the vendor smiled on the innocent child and explained that someone has to manage the puppet (with the invisible stings), it cannot dance on its own. Shrey got quite surprised and picked up another bit bigger puppet and expected it to dance, the same thing happened, his father explained that size does not matter and it will dance only when someone will make it dance, the movements of the puppet depends on the will and wish of the controller of the puppet.

Shrey got disheartened and wanted to buy the puppet with one condition only that it should dance on its own, but his father explained him again that puppets are puppets, they are made to dance only by their masters and preached him not to become a puppet in his life, his father explained that he should learn to take his own decisions, believe on his abilities and manage himself keeping the remote of his controls with himself only, his father further told him that he has worked with many people, who were just puppets in life, they walked, talked and danced as per the sweet will and wish of their masters and Shrey should not become a puppet in life.

Ability 9: Sticking on Your Principles and Doing your Duty

There is a direct correlation with your ethical principles and ethical success, if we stick to our principles and keep on doing our duties sincerely, even if no one is observing, no one on earth can stop us in succeeding. This concept can be understood better with the following thought provoking story of a King who learnt from a Saint who was ready to sacrifice his life for his duty and principles.

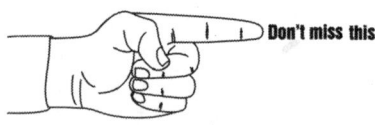
Don't miss this

The Saint and the Scorpion

This is a story of a king who learnt a lesson of his life from a saint who was ready to sacrifice his life for the call of his duty.

One day the king, who was waiting for his prey in the jungle observed a saint looking at a black scorpion walking on the branch of a tree over the river to cross it. Suddenly the scorpion trembled and fell into the river. The saint who was observing it carefully immediately rushed for its rescue and put his hand in the river to save it. The scorpion bit the saint and the saint immediately pulled his hand out of water and screamed in pain. A few seconds later again the saint extended his hand to save the scorpion, who was still struggling in the water to survive and again the same thing happened, the deadly Scorpion again bit the saint and this time it was so strong that the saint screamed loudly in pain. With the poison of the scorpion, the saint was almost on the verge of getting unconscious.

Again after a few minutes the saint gathered some courage and this time picked up the scorpion in the flowing river. The scorpion bit him again but the saint was able to pull it out of the water and placed it on the earth. This time the scorpion bite was so strong and poisonous that the saint nearly fainted.

'I am my favourite' is the statement of a confident person

The king who was watching the whole incident was shocked to see all this and rushed towards the saint who fell down on earth in acute pain. The bites of the scorpion were so deadly that white foam came out from the saint's mouth and the colour of his skin turned blue. It seemed that the saint would die in few minutes.

The king asked why he did it again and again to save the deadly Scorpion from drowning despite Scorpion's poisonous bites.

The saint replied : "The scropion, while drowning was not leaving his nature (of biting), then how as a saint can I forget my duty of helping others, I am a saint, it is my duty to save the life of others. He did his duty and I did mine."

The ability to stick to your guiding principles in all circumstances will make your character so strong that even if you do a mistake, others will ignore it. They will know you are a principled person and will never doubt your abilities.

Ability 10 : Self Confidence and Belief in Your Near and Dear Ones

Till the time you have confidence in yourself, your abilities and in your well-wishers, no one can stop you from being successful and happy. It is said that nothing succeeds like success.

To understand the level of 'confidence' enjoy the following story of a pupil who demonstrated the highest level of confidence in his guru.

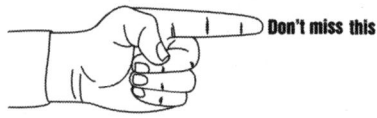

The Story of Confidence

Here is a short but amazing story of the confidence of a pupil in his guru (master or a saint).

There was a well-known guru who was famous for his teachings and exemplary conduct. He used to roam around in different villages to preach people. Villagers also respected him a lot and used to give him some gifts like eatables as a mark of respect and as a token of thanks.

One day when Guruji finished his sermon, a farmer came to pay his gratitude by offering him some cucumbers from his field. Guruji started eating the cucumbers which were very tasty. After having eaten a few, the another one that he picked up was so bitter, that Guruji could not even take a single bite.

He had never tasted anything bitter than that in his life before. He was about to spit and throw it away but inadvertently offered that bitter cucumber to his disciple who was sitting with him and studying (there is always a child in all of us and we all want to do some mischief to make our life interesting and happy). The disciple took the cucumber, thanked Guruji and started eating that bitter cucumber happily and surprisingly finished it without even saying a single word of bitterness.

Guruji was surprised that how his disciple finished the bitterest cucumber of which he could not even take a bite. Guruji asked his disciple about it.

Skilled Abilities

The disciple replied, "Gurudev, you have given me the best of the gifts of my life like self-recognition, knowledge, learning and I enjoyed all of them, today if you have given one bitter cucumber do you think I should complain. I finished it considering it as your gift and it did not taste bitter than. I have full confidence in you that you will never give me anything bad, which can harm me. Even this bitterness will help me in keeping my stomach clean, Thank You".

> *It is not the result of 100th hit of yours which breaks the rock; this is the result of those 99 efforts, which made the ground of this success*

Guruji was amazed with the answer and hugged him and gave countless blessings for his unmatched confidence in him.

If you ask me the present day success stories of confidence, I can give you many, where the people have shown a lot of confidence in themselves (self confidence) to be successful.

Take the case of **Russi Mody**, who joined Tata Steel as an office assistant in 1939 and became the Chairman and Managing Director of the company (1984-93). How can it be possible without a lot of confidence. Just see the other side of the coin also. **Mr. J. R. D. Tata** who supported him from one position to another and finally to the position of Chairman and Managing Director was also having a lot of confidence in Mody and that is why Mody could achieve those heights.

The superstar of Indian Film Industry, **Mr. Amitabh Bacchan** is not an exception to this fact. His career from a freight broker in a shipping firm in Calcutta to Superstardom in Mumbai, for where he was meant to be and he became the undisputed king of the Indian Film Industry, proved his ability to believe in himself and the unmatched self-confidence.

Another convincing example of self confidence is of KFC's - **Col. Sanders'**, who lost his father at the age of 6 and started supporting his family with his mother. He saw his successful business coming to an end at the age of 65 because of a Flyover constructed over his restaurant forcing his business to close and then thought of a new chicken recipe which almost became a rage, boosting his business and taking it to new heights. This is how Kentucky Fried Chicken was born.

Colonel Harland Sanders finally retired from the business when he was eighty years old due to illness but he proved to the world that if you are determined and believe in yourself, you can do anything any time.

The story of **Dhirubhai Ambani**, the Ex - Chairman of Reliance Industries (it was the only privately owned Fortune 500 Indian company at that time), is as exciting as any other success story in the world. Born in a village school teacher's family, started supporting his family from an early age by putting up onion/potato fries stall on weekends and could not continue his studies after matriculation due to poor economic condition. He went to Aden (Yemen) to work as a clerk and later as petrol pump attendant in Dubai. He dreamt and achieved his dream of becoming the owner of 'Vimal' and the 25 million ton oil refinery.

> *It is not the failure but the fear of failure, which prevents us to take action in life.*

Take the case of **Shivaji**, his confidence in himself and his great mother - Jijabai, who motivated and educated her son in such a way that Shivaji was able to make the golden history and become our idol.

Last but not the least, now I am going to give a brief description of one of the most famous personalities in the world. Although I am not disclosing his name right now; let us see a brief of his life then you can guess his name.

There was a man in America, who failed in business in 1831,

he was defeated for the legislature in 1832,

he failed in business in 1834,

Skilled Abilities

his sweetheart died in 1835,
he suffered a nervous breakdown in 1836,
he was defeated in an election again in 1838,
he again failed to win election in 1843,
and the success still was not for him when he lost election again in 1846,
again he was defeated for congress in 1848,
again he was defeated for the senate in 1855,
again was defeated for the vice-presidency in 1856,
and he was defeated again for the senate in 1858.

After all these failures for years together, he never gave-up and won the election for the post of **President of United States of America** in 1860. He was **Abraham Lincoln.**

Just think do we all have this self-confidence to struggle and win in life like Lincoln had? Are we so confident and sure that one day we will win and never give up like him? Actually this is one of the best practical examples of **Never... Never... Never give up.**

Point of View – Hanuman Syndrome

As far as the question of capabilities and skills are concerned, let me tell you that all of us are suffering with *Hanuman Syndrome,* which means we have all the powers with us but we are not aware of them as *Lord Hanuman* who was reminded about his powers by Jamwant. *Jamwant* told him that he can fly in the air, can jump the sea, can pick up any weight and can make impossible - possible.

The same thing is with us, we possess many qualities and powers but either we are not aware of them or have forgotten them completely. Rather I would say that we are born with a curse to forget all our abilities and powers and in our lifetime we need one *Jamwant* as a catalytic agent to wake us up and remind us about the powers we all possess. It may be a superb analytical ability, critical decision making, third sense presentation, innovativeness, creativity or any other CSFs (Critical Success Factors).

Management Lesson

A crow was sitting on a tree, doing nothing all day. A small rabbit saw the crow, and asked him, "Can I also sit like you and do nothing all day long? The crow answered «Sure, why not.» So, the rabbit sat on the ground below the crow, and rested. All of a sudden, a fox appeared, jumped on the rabbit and ate it.

Learnings from the Lesson:
To be sitting and doing nothing, you must be sitting very high up.

Whenever I get the Key to Success, someone changes the Lock.

4

INCULCATING PRODUCTIVE HABITS

(Sowing the Seed of Winning)

Habits can make you or break you...

There is a very interesting phrase that - habits can make you or break you. If you want to be successful in life, you have to have some positive, constructive and value adding habits of winning, You must have observed that sometimes apart from the winners, prizes are given to participants also to motivate them so that they also feel good and make it a habit to work harder and win in life. The foundation of any habit is a simple thought which becomes your destiny. Read the following lines to know how the destiny is in your hands.

Destiny

Sow Good Thoughts
Reap Good Actions

Sow Good Actions
Reap Good Habits

Sow Good Habits
Reap Good Character

Sow Good Character
Reap Good Destiny

Hence Your Destiny is in Your Hands...

Sometimes when we do not change our habits, we are bound to lose like the tree surrounded by an *'amar bail'* (*immortal vine* - a yellow, non-expiring, parasite vine).

Amar bail can ruin a full grown green and flourishing tree. It is said that the *amar bail* starts as a very small and undernourished vine, which is not even able to support itself for food. It takes the help of a fully-grown green tree and with the food and support of the tree, starts growing slowly and climbing towards the top of the tree. A day comes when the vine reaches at the top and flourishes itself in such a way that it covers all the leaves of the tree and stops the light to reach the tree and therefore the tree starts dying slowly. As the tree dies the *amar bail* grows continuously. A time comes when the green tree completely dies and as *amar bail* sucks it up fully but does not change its basic habit of not generating food for self and to take it from the tree. Now because the tree is no more living and cannot offer food to the *amar bail*, it also starts dying slowly and a day comes when both the green tree and the *amar bail* completely vanish.

Here some points are to be noted that both of them, the tree and the vine are not changing their basic habits and that is why they are bound to die quite early. The trees which do not offer food and do not support *amar Bail* live much longer. Here neither the *amar bail* is changing its habit of dependency on the tree for food and support nor the tree is changing its habit to give food and support the *amar bail* (depicting a bad habit) which is going to be the cause of its death one day because both of them are stubborn and do not wish to change for life.

Let us understand the value of habits in our life, we may also be having some *amar bail* type of destructive habits in our life which can even take our lives – these could be the habits of smoking, drinking, gambling or the more dangerous ones like negative thinking, sulking, criticising and procrastinating or in-action, which are taking us towards failure, ill health and ultimately towards total loss. Either you have to stop supporting these unproductive and killing habits or they will stop you to be successful.

$$\left\{ \text{First you make a habit and then the Habit makes you} \right\}$$

To be successful in life it is important to have some useful and productive habits, either you need to nourish existing positive habits or you need to inculcate productive habits. Let us see some positive and productive habits which can help us out in achieving our goals of life.

Productive Habits :

1) Never Criticise Anyone or Anything

If you see fools around you, don't lose your heart, you are there to rule over them, somebody has said it beautifully...

There is a common habit in almost all human beings and they enjoy this habit a lot. This is the most refreshing habit for them and they pass their precious and valuable time with great efforts in enjoying this fatal habit.

Yes, you are right, this habit is known as criticism. Most people love to criticise people, processes or systems, alternatively they can criticise anything they wish to, as and when they get the opportunity, anytime any day and anywhere.

The first productive habit we are going to learn today is **Not to Criticise Anyone or Anything.**

Criticism spoils our social relationships completely. We must make it a ground rule to note and keep on checking ourselves frequently to ensure that we are not enjoying criticism. We need to accept that no one and nothing is perfect in this world and we do not have any right to criticise. We might also be having a lot of shortcomings, we might not talk to people if they are not reasonable but criticism should be avoided in all circumstances.

> *If you see fools around you, don't lose your heart, you are there to rule over them.*

How an intelligent king managed and dealt with this issue can be learnt with the following story and you will learn how you feel and react when you stand in some other person's shoes, whom you are criticising.

Let us learn from the story of Hari who was suffering with the habit of criticism.

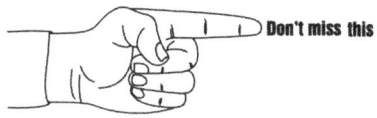

Hanging Sword

There was a scholar –Hari, who proved his mettle again and again and people respected him a lot for his achievements.

As we have discussed during the beginning of this chapter that there are some strong and some weak points with all of us, the same was the case with Hari also. He was also suffering from the disease of criticism.

One day the king of the state was roaming around in the city disguising himself in plane clothes so that people are not able to recognise him. He visited many public places and just listened to what people say about their state and about their king.

When he reached near a river where people were bathing and discussing on general topics he observed Hari talking on different matters in a flow. This attracted many intelligent people around him and the king too wanted to listen to him. He talked a lot about the basic amenities, the administration of the state, the amenities available to the citizens and the planning and execution flaws for implementation of welfare oriented policies.

As per his habit, he even started criticising the king and openly challenged the functioning and administration. He told that the king is so busy in himself in the palace that he is just not bothered about the irrigation stream from the river to their village. Others also joined him in criticising the king on these issues.

The king who was listening all this felt really sorry that he could not take care of the irrigation plans for their village but was also annoyed with Hari as he did not like this unproductive criticism. The king decided to deal with the issue in a very positive manner and left for his palace.

A messenger from king's palace reached Hari to invite him to the palace for some discussions with the king and the ministers on development and irrigation matters. Hari felt great and accepted the offer. He was feeling overjoyed as it was a mark of respect for him to be in the palace as the guest of the king and to discuss and advise on some important issues to the king himself.

On reaching the king's palace Hari was given a red carpet treatment but he was excited to meet the king and wanted to see the palace from inside as he had heard a lot about the artistic beauty of the palace. Minutes later a minister himself greeted Hari and told him to have food before he meets the king and the council of ministers.

> **Don't wait for the iron to be hot to start striking, start striking to make it hot.**

Hari was feeling very hungry and was anxious to taste the food of the palace, which was prepared by the best of the chefs in the state. An overenthusiastic Hari was taken to one of the beautiful huge dining rooms of the palace where different types of dishes were waiting for him. He was amused to see such palatable food with a huge variety. The fragrance was increasing Hari's hunger and he just wanted to have the food without wasting even a single minute. The minister escorting Hari requested him to have his food and informed Hari that they will be back soon.

Hari thanked the minister, who left for some work. Now it was the time for Hari to have the most delicious food he had ever seen in his life. He sat on the beautiful golden chair of the dinning table to have the food.

When Hari was about to start the food, he saw a sword - hanging from the roof on his head, tied with a thin thread. Hari got terrified and thought that if the sward falls on his head, he may die. He decided to leave the chair as early as possible so that he is safe. So he quickly finished his meal, left the chair and came out of the dining room.

After some time the king himself came with the minister and met Hari and asked about the food. Hari could not answer in detail and just said that the food was good, actually he somehow finished the food and was not able to comment on the taste in details.

The king asked someone to bring the food from the dinning room and asked Hari to taste some of the dishes again. Hari did that and was surprised that dishes were tasteless because of absence of salt but their presentation was good.

The king asked Hari why he was not able to comment on the dishes earlier and why he did not tell the king that there is no salt in any of the dishes he tasted.

Hari had to tell him the truth and described how his attention was not on the food but on the hanging sword only, which was hanging right on his head with a thin thread when he was on the dinning table. The food, its presentation and taste, etc. were minor issues and he wanted to save his life first, that is why he never gave any attention on the food and just came out without having much and without tasting it properly.

The king laughed a lot and told Hari that the same thing even applies to king also. He told Hari that many swords are hanging on his head too, to name a few - security of the state from the neighboring states, the preventive actions in case of droughts and floods, collection of taxes for treasury and other important issues relating to administration of vital importance. The issues like pulling streams from rivers for all villages are not that much in high priority as these are the duties of the municipal corporations of the area and that is why he had appointed different ministers for different jobs.

Hari immediately understood the whole issue and came to know that he has been called here to realise his mistake of criticism. He felt sorry for his behaviour and was impressed with the way the king has taught him this practical lesson.

The king laughed and appointed him as the inspector of civil amenities of his area as he was an able and intelligent person who knew what is to be done. Hari was pleased, he thanked the king and returned to his home with the following message.

> "Never criticise anyone, as you are not standing in their shoes so you do not know from which hardship someone is going, what the real circumstances are and what are the preferences. The importance of different works for different people can be different and cannot be measured on any one yardstick. To enjoy your life with best relationships with others, never criticise anyone."

In a few days only Hari was able to pull a stream for his village from the river with the help of the civil administration of his area. He learnt a lesson that instead of criticising invest your time and efforts in 'doing' something and make the difference.

2) Acknowledging Others and Saying Thank You

Just ponder on one achievement without the help of other people around us. How can we be successful without getting their help? Our family members and closed ones help us in almost every aspect of life. For example taking the example to lead a normal life our mother or wife helps us not only in household things but work outside also to support the family, our fathers or husbands, apart from earning, help us for outside household works such as shopping, guiding or anything, our teachers help in acquiring knowledge, our mentors for our attitude and skill, our companies for advancing in careers and why should we forget the Government - supporting us with the social setup including electricity, water and waste management, etc. Do you think we can live our life like Robinson Crusoe living on a lonely island where there is no one to help? The answer is 'No', we cannot dream and think our life without others' help. Now the question is what do we do for our helpers? Sometimes we even do not thank them.

Thanking anybody and everybody who is helping you is the second productive habit we need to inculcate as early as possible; this will surely fetch very positive results.

On a lighter side, let us see how monkeys conveyed their thanks to a hat seller.

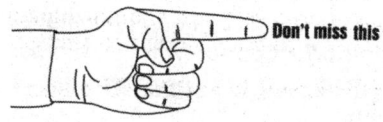

Grand Father

It's an old story that we read in our childhood but this time it is with a new ending.

A hat-seller who was passing by a forest decided to take a nap under one of the trees, so he left his whole basket of hats by the side. A few hours later, he woke up and realised that all his hats were gone. He looked up and to his surprise, the tree was full of monkeys and they had taken all his hats.

The hat seller started thinking how he can get the hats back, while he was thinking he started scratching his head. The next moment, the monkeys imitated him and started scratching their heads. Next, he took off his hat; the monkeys imitated again and took off their hats.

An idea came to Hat seller's mind, he threw his hat on the earth and the monkeys did that too. He quickly collected all hats from the earth and managed to escape by saying thanks to monkeys.

Fifty years later, hat seller's grandson also became a hat-seller and heard this monkey story from his grandfather. One day, just like his grandfather, he was passing by the same forest. It was very hot, and he took a nap under the same tree and left the hats on the ground. He woke up and realised that all his hats were taken by the monkeys on the tree.

He remembered his grandfather's story and started scratching his head, all the monkeys imitated him and started scratching their heads too. He removed his hat and fanned himself for air and again the monkeys followed, they also removed their hats and started fanning themselves. Now, very convinced of his grandfather's idea, the hat-seller threw his hat on the earth thinking that monkeys will imitate him and will do so but to his utmost surprise, the monkeys still held on to all the hats.

Then one monkey climbed down the tree, grabbed the Hat-seller's hat from the ground, took it to the tree back and shouted THANK YOU and asked,-"You think only you had a grandfather !!!???"

3) Accepting Your Mistakes and Feeling Sorry

We are not perfect and we cannot be, we will mess up some times and will repeat mistakes, we are bound to do some mistakes and bound to fail in some attempts, we may disappoint someone, hurt someone and we may not come upto somebody's expectations. It is OK with all of us, we are not a super computer, it is OK to fail sometimes and it is OK to do mistakes, only the person who keeps trying will do some mistakes, it is the part and parcel of life.

Now what to do after messing up, just feel sorry, and say loudly to the person you have messed with, people are generous, they forgive and forget, even if they don't it is not your fault, you just need to inculcate the habit of saying **'sorry'** for any mistake you have done, even if inadvertently.

> *Your value goes up by saying sorry and you become greater by helping others.*

On the lighter side, there is a phrase that 'Only Donkeys do not feel Sorry'(because they never realise they have done a mistake) and that is why they remain donkeys only, let us see how donkeys remain donkeys only.

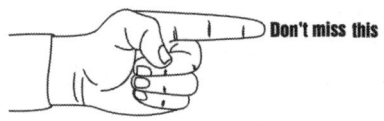
Don't miss this

Donkeys will be Donkeys

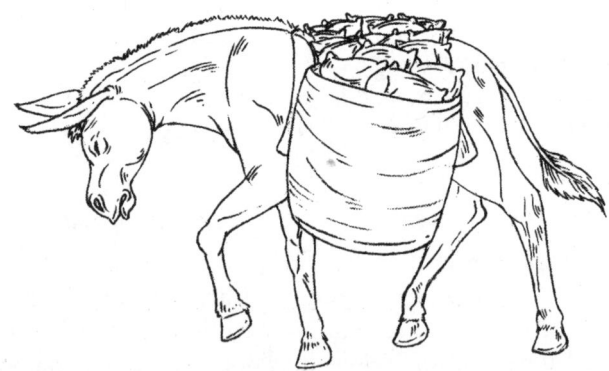

There was a trader and he used to sell salt to other cities. He had a number of donkeys to transport his salt from one city to another. The donkeys were expected to cross a small stream to reach another city.

One day while crossing the stream a donkey slipped into the water and a lot of salt on its back got diluted in the water quickly. After this the donkey felt quite light and thought of adopting this technique again and again to reduce its burden.

When the trader observed that a particular donkey has learned the technique to reduce his burden, he changed his plan and in place of putting the salt he started loading cotton on that donkey's back.

The donkey was a donkey and could not distinguish between white salt and white cotton and adopted the same technique of slipping in water. This time the water reached the cotton, got soaked and became even heavier.

When the donkey observed for a few days that this technique was increasing its load, it stopped doing it and the trader started loading the salt again.

That is why somebody has said rightly ... Donkeys will be Donkeys.

4) Helping Others and Getting Helped

In our social setup helping each other only can help all of us in achieving our goals. I cannot forget the days when I used to spend more than 10 hours every day in Delhi Public Library, Sarojini Nagar, New Delhi and about 2 hours for physical endurance with a dream to become an IPS Officer. How can I forget many seniors who could clear civil services exams and helped us out in knowing how to crack these All India Level Competitive Exams. Describing what they told us and how could we use their advices may deviate us from the main subject of helping others but there I learnt the art of selfless help for others. If people around you are successful, the satisfaction you get to see others happy and successful when you helped them out makes you even happier. I do not feel any hesitation in saying that the formula of happy life is to help others and get helped in our endeavours.

Getting help from others...

Have you heard the phrase – 'Only Crying Baby Gets the Milk', what does it mean.

You need to ask for help yourself otherwise how others will come to know that you need help. They may not come to help you out, asking for help is not demeaning and not at all bad and that is why our 4th productive habit is helping others and getting helped.

Asking for help from your boss, subordinates, colleagues and peers in office or from your spouse, kids and parents at home is not at all bad and rather they feel comfortable when you ask for their help, it is a natural tendency and you should make use of this productive habit.

When you expect for some help from your kids, they feel happy and get the impression that they are intelligent enough to help you out.

The only important point to keep in mind before using this productive habit is to take care that you ask for help only when you really need it and you cannot proceed further without that. If asking for help means getting others to do your job, it can fail miserably and may produce opposite results.

Let us enjoy the story of Alex who helped his pupil John in becoming a world class boxer, what happened to them is a lesson to learn.

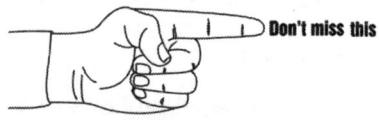

Don't miss this

The Story of Boxers

There was a great boxer Alex, who won many championships, got many medals and awards and started his boxing academy to locate and train new boxers.

There was a poor boy - John, who used to help the boxers in day to day works as helping them to get their gloves, training kits and towels for which John got tips. John also got interested in boxing and thought of becoming a boxer in future. When Alex observed John's interest, he asked John, who expressed his inability to pay the fees because of his poor financial

condition. Alex was impressed with John's dedication towards boxing and offered him to join his academy without paying any fees.

Both John and Alex worked very hard and Alex taught best of the techniques to John as he wanted to see his pupil - John as a champion. The destiny played its role and highly paying Challengers Trophy Championship was announced in which both Alex and John participated and surprisingly reached the finals. John was in a fix before the final bout with his coach Alex, he thought a lot if he should stand against his coach in finals or not and if he should fight naturally to win the bout or should he lose the final to honour his coach.

What would you have done if you would have been in John's place?

On the day of the final bout both of them were standing in front of each other and were ready to prove their mettle. There was a huge crowd and people were shouting at the highest levels of the pitch. Some of them were supporting Alex and some cheering for John.

John fought very well and was ultimately declared the champion. John's dream was fulfilled and he was very happy after beating his coach and teacher Alex. He got a lot of money, name and fame after winning this championship. Alex after facing the defeat left the city for good and settled in some other state, where?, John did not know ever.

Years passed by and John grew old, he was now the Mayor of the city. He earned a lot of respect being the 'Champion' in his life. One day John came to know that his coach who left the state 20 years back is coming back to meet John. He was very happy and asked his children and wife to give a red carpet treatment to his master. John was thankful to Alex because he was the person who made his life, taught him boxing with which he was able to gain money, name and fame in life.

Alex came to John's house and was received very well by John's family. In Alex's honour John threw a huge party and called all the big personalities and celebrities. Alex was also very happy and shared all old stories with everyone over there.

After the party Alex was with John and his family and they were chit chatting, during the discussion suddenly Alex asked a very interesting question from John about the happiest moment of John's life?

John was caught unexpected, but came up with the truth that the happiest moment of his life was when he beat Alex in the ring in the final of Champion's trophy. John also disclosed that it was his dream to beat Alex in the ring.

If you would have been in John's place, would you have shared that beating your coach was your happiest day?

As soon as Alex listened to this he laughed uncontrollably, he laughed so loudly that all the family members turned their attention on the subject matter. Alex was laughing continuously and somehow controlled himself and asked John laughingly, "John do you really think you beat me up that day".

Alex was not able to control his laughter and the level of embarrassment for John was pretty high. John slowly said, "Yes Alex I think so". Alex who was continuously laughing stopped laughing and observed all the family members of John looking towards him only. He told John to change the topic, as he was not willing to talk on this matter in the presence of his family members.

John who was not feeling very comfortable insisted Alex to clarify why he laughed and what is the reason of his not sharing some information in front of his family members. Alex again requested John to change the topic but John insisted again and again.

Alex got serious and became quiet. He kept quiet for a while and told John in a very sad voice that 25 years back his father took some loan for business and lost all the money and with this shock died under the burden of repaying. Now the entire burden came on Alex's shoulders and it was not practically possible for Alex to repay the loan amount even in next 20 years. He continuously thought for the solution but nothing came out. During that time only the Challengers Trophy Championship was announced and he took part in to make some money. He was sure of his victory, which could get him some cash reward too but it was just 25 % of the total loan amount. He was under pressure to arrange more money, which was now his first priority. He was very much conscious for the education and upbringing of his children and knew that even if he pays all money he had, he just can't settle the loan and this will negatively impact his family and children.

At that time only, one of the Bookies contacted him and told him that there is a bet speculation on his bout with John and the rate is 1: 20 which means that there is a surety of Alex winning the bout as he is the coach of John and can beat John easily. Now the bookie told him that he can bet one million on John provided Alex promise to lose the bout because in that case he will win 20 million dollars and will give 10 million to Alex for losing the bout. He gave 24 hours to Alex to think on the proposition and asked him to call him back for his decision.

Alex got annoyed with the bookie in the beginning and asked that bookie to stop this nonsense, he told the bookie that he has never lost any bout and the question of losing the bout against his pupil does not arise at all. When he calmed down he thought a lot and somehow came to the conclusion that for the well-being of his family and for the future of his children, he will lose the bout and will repay the loan with 10 million USD and will leave this place for good as he cannot face the people after losing the bout to his pupil.

> Emotionally intelligent people are not the wind changers, they are the winds.

Knowing this, John got shocked. He could not utter even a single word and it seemed to him as he has lost everything in life and nothing is remaining. The air castle he made was broken into dust and he lost everything he gained in years. He thought he was the best and people respected him for that. He earned a lot of money and gained respect for being a national champion but the reality was something else.

If you would have been in the place of Alex, would you have shared this information with your pupil after 20 years, that too in front of his family, who always thought that John was the best?

Tears rolled down on John's cheeks and he could not utter anything and couldn't believe he never won but Alex lost and that too for money to support his family. John told him that this win was the base on which he was enjoying his life, he became the mayor of the city because people respected him to be a champion and now there is nothing to enjoy and celebrate. His happiness of life was shattered and he felt ashamed in front of his family members.

That night was the toughest night John had ever spent, absolutely sleepless and restless. He kept on thinking the whole night about the reality and thought that the castle of his life was standing on false pillars of somebody's helplessness.

He could not understand if Alex helped him in getting the biggest happiness or biggest sadness of his life.

Swami Vivekananda has said, "Wake up, get up and don't stop until you reach your Goal."

5) Learning New Traits

I am sure you must have heard the phrase that everyone is a learner for life, you keep on learning new things in life and your learning and adaptable attitude is the key to success. Always request people to teach you something positive and productive. Learning new techniques in new areas will pave the path of your success. You should not only learn from your seniors rather sometimes the best learnings come from juniors as they are very apt in what they are doing.

This is possible only when you accept that 'I don't know but I can learn'. I feel many people can't even accept that they don't know in any circumstances, upto the time you accept that you don't know something, how will you learn.

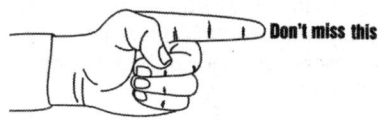

Eklavya's Story

Once upon a time there was a boy -'Eklavya', who wanted to become the best archer of the world, he wanted to learn the art of archery from the best of the master at that time – 'Guru Dronacharya' but could not do so. Do you know what he did? He made a statue of his 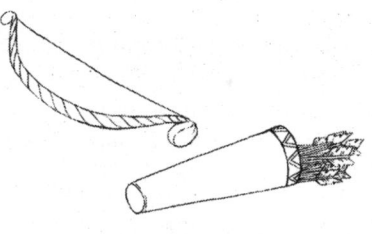 *Guru and asked his statue if he can teach him and started practising archery. One day Guru Dronacharya himself saw his excellent archery, he was amazed to see his skills and asked him who his Guru was. Eklavya took him to Guru Dronacharya's statue and said that this was his guru. Guru Dronacharya was committed to the promise done to Bhishma Pitamah to make their clan the best in warfare and binding to that oath, he expected Eklavya's right thumb as his 'Guru Dakshina' (teaching fee), which Eklavya gave him happily and became an immortal name in Indian History.*

How amazingly Eklavya could become the best archer by asking his Guru's statue.

6) Praising Others

Each one of us is a package of good and bad habits. If we love someone, we tend to see all positives in that person and praise their positive habits to reinstate the fact that the person is lovable in our eyes and proving others about your smartness that you love a smart person. If we hate someone we see all negatives, and we keep on criticising those we do not like. This gives us the satisfaction of our right decision to hate them.

A very interesting fact about human behaviour is present in all age groups and in all circumstances. Everybody likes to be praised - be it an infant, adolescent, teenager, adult, mature or old person. We feel good if someone praises us and bond very fast with them and hate those who criticize us. We can use the mantra of praising for bonding with others.

Let us enjoy the story of two pots and learn how with the help of the habit of praising others the farmer could motivate a cracked pot.

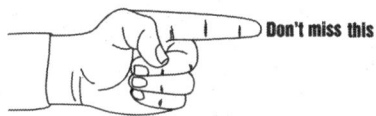

Don't miss this

2 Pots

It is a story of two pots of a farmer. The farmer was not having any facility to irrigate his field and used to bring water from a nearby

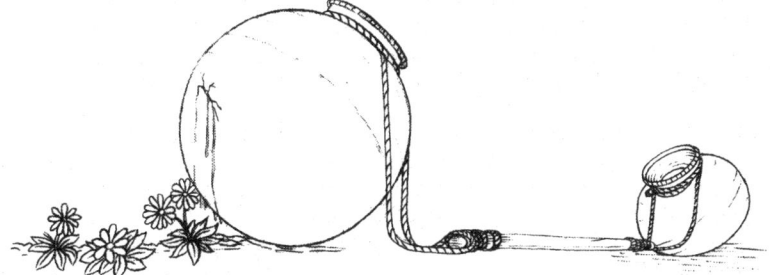

river in two pots tied to one big stick on both the sides and use to water the crops in his field.

One day one of the pots got smashed with a rock and got a crack. The water started leaking out from the pot and got wasted during the journey. The farmer used to fill both the pots from the river but only half the water would reach the field. This was the matter of tension for the cracked pot and it lost its heart and started suffering from inferiority complex that it is of no use to the farmer anymore and there is no value of its life to anyone.

When the farmer observed that the cracked pot is suffering with inferiority complex, he started praising the cracked pot to maintain its motivation by saying that even if it is cracked, it is carrying the water beyond its capacity to support him and that is why the farmer is very much thankful to the cracked pot. With such praising the cracked pot got a lot of motivation and kept on carrying water up to its maximum limit possible.

The farmer did not replace the cracked pot. The spring came and everyone was amused to see beautiful flowers in the desert. These were in the shape of a long line and surprisingly they were only on one side of the path.

The farmer was happy as this happened due to leaking water from the cracked pot. The cracked pot was also amazed to understand that life is not a waste as it could also contribute in making this earth a beautiful place.

What have we learnt from this story –praising can motivate someone to the level of best possible performance and it can help in achieving tasks which sometimes seems to be impossible in normal circumstances. Make it your habit to praise all those who are concerned with us, you never know what miracle you can see people doing whom you have praised.

7) *Taking Initiative*

This amazing habit of taking initiative can take you miles on the path of success. When you show interest, learn new things, accept new responsibilities and take initiative – you succeed, almost automatically. To understand this concept, let us read an interesting story of three friends.

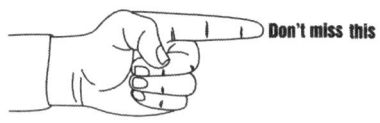

Initiative of Friends

There were three friends, who studied MBA together and eventually landed up in the same bank as colleagues. After about 3 years they observed that everything was good with them except one thing, despite same qualifications and experience their salaries varied. Where the first friend was getting a low salary, the second friend almost got double than the first one and the third friend was almost on triple of what first one got. There was a natural jealousy among the three.

One day when they observed that the differences in their salaries is creating a rift in their friendship they decided to approach their manager and asked the reason of differences in their salaries. The manager smiled and promised them to tell the reason but before that he wanted a report to be sent to headquarters urgently and told them to bring the budget sheet of last year to him so that they can make this year's budget and can send it to the headquarters.

The first friend kept on searching the file of budget in his computer but could not locate it. He searched with different names in all folders, searched all mails from his boss to him and his replies to his boss, searched every hard copy and eventually failed in locating the file. He called his boss and asked his help to send him last year's budget so that he can start working on future budget. His searching took one precious hour of his work.

The second friend was quite systematic, he was knowing where he has saved his budget file. He immediately looked to his 'Budget' folder in 'my documents', got the file, took a print and took it to his manager for his comments and further work.

The third one was very systematic and professional, he not only searched his file rather edited it by adding another column of this year budget, named it properly, applied a formula of 15 % addition in all incomes and revenues, removed the expenses not taking place this year, added new income company started getting this year and took this updated sheet to his manager to take his further guidance if the manager needs any changes before sending it to the headquarters.

The manager was very happy with the updated output excel sheet of the third friend and felt almost no need to correct it further. He called all three of them to show this work and explained that first difference in their salaries is because of their inclination and interest in their work. The second and third friend could locate the file easily because they kept it systematically and sincerely.

He further elaborated that another reason of difference in their salaries is the initiative and attitude. The third friend was not told to help his boss but he took initiative in making this year's budget. He deleted whatever was not required, added what was essential to be there, added a formula for automatic increase for this year and came for the final advise of his boss. Actually he did most of the work for his boss and left the boss without any burden.

All the three friends understood the reason of the differences in their salaries. Have you also understood why there is a difference in your salary in comparison to others?

8) Eating Right Food

Some people eat to live but some live to eat. You are in which category, if you are in first category, you can skip this chapter further but if you are in second category, you need to read it and understand it in detail.

A healthy mind can live only in a healthy body. It is important for you to give proper attention towards your mental and physical health for a successful life. Physical health directly contributes to your overall development.

I have personally seen people who know nothing about their food habits and do not know what to eat, how to eat and when to eat. They take a lot of junk food not knowing the side effects and even offer the same to their kids.

I am sorry to be very blunt here in mentioning that you are fooled by a lot of advertisements of junk foods, chips and soft drinks. Many companies try to attract consumers with the help of advertisements of their products which are being endorsed by cricketers, bollywood stars and other famous personalities. Some parents challenge that how can you keep your kids away from this type of food when everyone is eating it. It is reasonable and understandable if your kids have junk food once in a while, if as a habit you offer them something which can be make available in just 2 minutes, you are not doing a mistake, you are doing a crime.

Practice before you preach, is the mantra I have always believed in. I have faced the same challenge with my kids. Let me explain how we managed this in our home first.

> *Junk food, which may be liked by your Lips will always remain with your Hips.*

My son Shrey and daughter Shreshtha (Shiny) have a choice of any pizza once a month. They know that they can have one pizza of their choice just once in a month so they do not ask for it again and again and they understand why (we have made them understand), but to set this system, we had to sacrifice also. Me and my wife Jyoti loved pizzas a lot but when it is the question of your health and your family's health, we made some basic health rules for our house. This was highly appreciated and admired by Shrey's swimming coach – Mr. Gaurav Sharma (Ahlcon International School, Mayur Vihar).

We shared this concept with many people like Shrey's Principal – Mr. Ashok Pandey and Head Mistress – Mrs. Promila Mehta, they also appreciated this concept and even shared this with other parents and students.

Junk food is not only in western, oriental or continental cuisines, it can be in Indian foods like samosas, bread pakoras, etc. Although we are not against these foods completely but maintaining a balance between the healthy and junk food is not only important for a healthy body but is also required for a healthy mind.

My Yoga Teacher and Mentor – Ram Chandra Ahlawat Sir always says:

Food – half, water - double, laughing – triple and playing / exercising – quadruple (4 times) will make you healthy, wealthy and wise. He has always advocated both physical and mental health and a beautiful balance of both, if one shakes the other cannot remain stable.

Although I am not against non vegetarians but I always prefer vegetarian food. It is simple, healthy and easy to digest, where you need about 6-8 hours in digesting the complex foods like non vegetarian, you just need 4-6 hours in digesting the vegetarian food. You just need to know that raw / uncooked food is the best, when you do not cook anything and take it in natural form. The results are amazing, the nutritious values are the highest in salads and uncooked vegetables and fruits.

> Sow the seed of a good Habit, you will have a Tree of Success soon.

The salads and sprouts are also known as simple foods and the food cooked with a lot of masalas (spices) are known as complex foods.

The simple food will make your life – simple.

The Magic of Water Therapy :

When I was preparing for civil services with a dream to become an IPS officer, I met some amazing people in DPL Sarojini Nagar, I may not be remembering their names but they taught me about the water therapy which keeps your body clean and strong. Once I adopted therapy I always practised it. I even shared it in my Internal Security Academy (Police Training) with my batch-mates and trainers and they appreciated that. Some of them already knew about it and were familiar with the positive and amazing results.

Water therapy is very simple, you just need to take two steps to remain healthy :

1) Take at least 2 glasses of fresh water (normal temperature) before going to bed.
2) Take 2 to 3 glasses of water after getting up (even before brushing your teeth and before going to washroom).

This will not only clear your system but will keep you healthy throughout your life. You will not face any stomach ailments (which is the power house for body) and your mind will be cool and fresh. You just need to keep one thing in mind that the water should be of normal temperature and should not be very hot or cold (however in winters you can take a little warm water).

Another important point in food habits is the **intake time of fruits**. Generally I have seen people taking it after the food, which is quite not that healthy and useful, let me tell you how.

Fruits are simple foods and just take less than 4 hours in getting digested, whereas cooked food takes about 6-7 hours. So if you have taken the cooked food, it is sitting in your intestines for 6-7 hours stopping the path of fruits if taken after the meal. Fruits will start fermenting the food en route and will not solve any purpose, it is like sending a jet plane after a bullock-cart in a narrow lane (intestines), it is bound to crash.

Now let us see if we reverse the pattern what will happen. If you take fruits before the meal (i.e. empty stomach) it will take lesser time for fruits to get digested and it will keep your intestines empty for the food to come. This way you will be sending a jet in a empty lane first and when it will fly off, you can send now a bullock cart which will take some time.

I am sure you have understood that the right time to take the fruits is before the meals.

Another thing we need to take care is the **temperature of food and drinks** we are taking. Body eventually makes everything hot inside it, Taking a lot of cold foods or drinks can disturb the body temperature. Taking hot and cold food items or drinks on close succession are also harmful for the body but surprisingly in fast food joints, people take hot burgers with cold drinks, which is very harmful (at least in Indian conditions).

Taking food made of crops grown on high pesticides is equally dangerous, naturally grown food with no or least quantity of pesticides (**Organic Food**) is far healthy and good for body (and surely for mind too).

People depend a lot on **Canned Food and Canned Juices** thinking they are 'Real', anything which is canned can be kept away from fermentation with the help of preservers only, with these type of canned food / juices these preservers enter in our body and start preserving the food we otherwise take, which is just the reverse process what body does with food, body starts fermenting the food and preservers start preserving it, this fight inside the body is also very bad for our health as the food should be digested naturally inside the body and should never be stopped by preservers, which have entered in our body through 'unreal' canned food / drinks.

Management Lesson

There was a very good HR Manager, he recruited many employees for his company and kept on checking if they were happy or not, once he recruited a high achiever who was very demanding. After about a week of his recruitment, the HR manager approached the demanding high performer and checked his well-being and asked him how he was and if he is happy and satisfied in the company.

The high achiever was probably waiting for the moment and blasted the HR Manager with his frustration, he explained why he was not happy in the company because he has not got his Identity Card, he is not sure of his PF and Gratuity forms being properly filled, the air conditioner was not functional in his office, one roller of his chair was broken, the light was not adequate and he was not able to get cold water, had to wait for his turn to get his choice of tea / coffee and so on and so forth...

The HR Manager said – "oh, this is so sad, but this is just the question of one month".

The high performer happily asked the HR Manager if he will solve all these problems in a month.

The HR manager replied – "No I cannot solve any of them, but you will be Habitual by then.

To Err is Human but to forgive is Not the company policy.

LEAD TO SUCCEED

(Leading from the Front)

Ordinary people doing extraordinary activities and producing amazing results are known as Leaders.

If anyone has to pick up a single most trait in personality which will make him / her successful for sure; it will be leadership. If you have got leadership qualities, no one on this earth can stop you in achieving the success you want in life.

It means you need to be a leader to be successful – Yes, you need to be, by all means, now the question - Are leaders born or are they made ?

Try to answer the above question before going through the details below.

The answer is 'both' (Leaders are born and they are made too), some people are born with leadership qualities (by birth) as they are god gifted.

But in many cases, people are not born as leaders and there may be very few leadership qualities in them, but they can still become leaders by acquiring leadership qualities.

Let us understand the phenomenon of **'Made Leader'** with the help of a story. There was a boy in Gujarat who went to London for higher studies and become a Barrister but could not address public at all. He has written in his book that he initially could never gather enough courage to speak in public but later in his life he did wonders and become a leader the world remembered for ever - can you guess his name. He was – Mohan Das Karamchand (Mahatma) Gandhi, who has written these facts in his autobiography – 'My Experiments with Truth'.

> Leaders are born and they are made too, you are surely a born leader and you can be made a Great Leader.

What is Leadership ?

The ability or efficiency to influence or divert a group of people to change their behavioural patterns and leading them to different directions to achieve predetermined goals is leadership.

Leadership is the process of influencing an individual or a team to do something that they would otherwise not do. Effective leadership qualities grow with practice. It can be taught and learned.

Do we get leaders only in politics

While taking MBA classes and in many seminars whenever I have asked participants to give me some names of the leaders of the world, the most common names were of political leaders and generally the participants missed out players, actors, spiritual leaders and business leaders and leaders with negative thoughts. Just to avoid any controversy, I am not mentioning any names here but there are many leaders who possessed all leadership traits but their goals may be negative. Coming back to the positive leadership traits, we can say Kapil Dev, Sunil Gavaskar, Sachin Tendulkar and MS Dhoni are leaders in Cricket, Amitabh Bacchan, Hritik Roshan and Kareena Kapoor are leaders in entertainment industry, PRS Oberoi, Ratan Tata, N R Naranmurthy, Asim Premjee and Ambani Brothers (Mukesh and Anil) are leaders in Business arena and Swami Ramdev and Aacharya Balkrishna are leaders on spiritual side.

Can you locate the common factor among all the above mentioned leaders – the common factor is the great followership they have. Actually **great followers make great leaders.**

Leadership Qualities

As we have seen in the beginning of the chapter that some people are born leaders and they possess some inborn leadership qualities from childhood, some are made leaders and they acquire all the leadership qualities with the passage of time. Both these types of leaders are socially, physically or intellectually stronger and different than rest of the people. They command leadership positions, they head the sports or cultural teams, they participate in debates and speeches, they impress others with their personality or knowledge, they are keen learners and acquire new skills quickly, their communication is effective and result oriented, they are mentally stronger than others. And in some cases their physical endurance surpasses others by miles but the most common trait will be their – **'Followers'**, you will find people following them, imitating them and listening to them, these types of leaders are generally addressed as **charismatic leaders.** They possess a charisma to impress others with their inborn or acquired abilities.

A very interesting fact about them is that they are highly flexible as per the situations and change as per the time and requirement. They are not very rigid and do not stuck to their believes in different situations. They are people's person and listen to them, they do not only teach and train others but being keen learners learn from them too.

Out of these many qualities of leaders, let us understand few qualities which can be learnt to be an effective leader.

{ *Great followers makes great leaders.* }

1. Self Confidence

If you believe in yourself then only others will believe you. Self confidence is the first key to leadership which ultimately leads you to success.

If you think you can, it is your thinking, but if you believe you can, you surely can.

2. Dream and Vision

You need to have a dream with a vision to achieve and accomplish, a football match without goal posts is useless, the dream should be big enough to motivate you and practical enough to accomplish. Leader is a torch bearer and his job is to enlighten the path of success for the followers.

Losers have dreams, winners have execution powers too.

3. High Level of Ambition, Passion and Energy to Achieve Dreams.

The ambition to achieve the dreams and goals is what drives someone to become a leader, the unmatched passion and non-ending energy is required to acquire these dreams. During this journey of achieving and realising your goals, you will face many challenges, people may criticise and de-motivate you, but self confidence, which is the first quality of Leadership will play very critical role in helping you to proceed further without getting hurt.

> *Make you passion – your profession, you will surely be successful in corporate world.*

4. Subject Knowledge and General Knowledge

Leaders possess a strong hold not only in the subject matter they are dealing with but on the general knowledge also. They know what is happening around them and in the world and they strategise, plan and execute accordingly expecting all challenges forehand and being ready with the probable solutions.

> *Ordinary people doing extraordinary activities and producing amazing results are known as leaders.*

Going against the stream is not always a very good idea, setting your sails as per the wind will lead you towards your goal.

5. The Desire to Lead and Power of Decision Making.

If you do not mind when someone criticises you. If you do not fumble if someone attacks on your views or philosophy and if you do not bother what people say about you, then you are a right material to be a leader. Otherwise you need to inculcate a habit of accepting all these challenges and adverse situations. You need to have a burning desire to lead and should expect people to challenge you so that you can raise the bar of your efforts. You should have a strong competition, which ensures your best side forward to face all challenges. The other unmatched ability of a leader is decision making. I have dedicated a full chapter on decision making so that this can be learnt and understood without any shadow of doubt.

6. Strategic Planning and Flawless Execution

No one has and no one will achieve success without strategic planning and seamless execution. The leaders have this quality, they can plan keeping all odds in mind. Their plan includes the 2nd and 3rd option if 1st does not work. They do not lose heart if they are not successful in the beginning as leadership is a long-term phenomenon, although short-term successes can become the stepping stones of motivation for a long-term success. Not only strategic planning but flawless execution is also required to pave the way for success which requires a lot of dedication, sincerity and perseverance.

7. Change Lovers

Leaders are change lovers, they love bringing positive changes and work hard to achieve their goals. People follow them for positive changes they can bring in their lives. This is the reason why many kids have posters of their favourite player or cricketer in their bedroom so that they get inspiration to change as per their role model.

On a lighter side, let us see the leadership qualities of an intelligent dog :

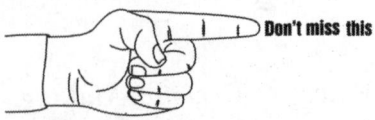 Don't miss this

The Leadership Qualities of a Dog

One day a dog lost his way in the jungle. Suddenly it saw a lion coming towards him. He did not lose heart and started thinking of saving his life. He observed some bones nearby and sat near the bones keeping his back towards the lion. Then he picked up a bone and started chewing it saying loudly – 'Wow, these lions taste the best, no other meat is as tasty as that of a lion. If I get one more lion, it will be a great day'.

The dog grumbled strongly and kept on chewing the bones continuously saying the same thing again and again.

The lion got confused, he thought that the dog was a lion eater, and he should run away to save his life. So the lion disappeared from there.

A monkey sitting on a tree was watching everything. He thought, this is the right time, if I explain everything to the lion, he will become my friend and I will be able to rule the jungle. The monkey ran after the lion, although the dog saw him running towards the lion and understood the whole story.

The monkey told the lion, how the dog had fooled him.

The lion got annoyed with the dog, and asked the monkey to accompany him to finish the dog. Monkey sat on the lion's back and they moved towards the dog.

Can you imagine the presence of mind of the dog and how it managed this situation.

As soon as the dog observed the lion coming with monkey on his back he understood the whole story. He again sat keeping his back towards the lion and started saying – "This Monkey is really useless, full one hour has passed and he could not manage even a single lion".

This again terrified the lion and he thought the monkey has laid a trap to capture him. He killed the monkey and ate it.

Moral of the story:

There are many such monkeys around us, try to identify them....
Never underestimate yourself, keep yourself focused....you are what you pretend to be.
If hope ends, there is nothing you could ever think of being yourself, so keep your hopes alive.

Types of Leaders

When I decided to become a leader (a gazetted police officer) and reached at Internal Security Academy for Police Training, I asked myself a very interesting question that what type of leader I want to become. A leader who is dominating or friendly, authoritative or democratic, should people fear me or should they respect me from heart. It was a question of becoming Hitler or Gandhi.

I am sure you must be having these questions in your mind too, you would be looking towards deciding the type of leadership you want and the guaranty of success associated with this type.

There are many types of leaders, you need to judge and decide, what type suites you for your prospective, challenge, and situation. The following types of leaders are more successful and these leadership styles can be learnt with sincere practice.

- **Creative Leaders**

Creative leaders take initiatives and start something new. Others may not have done these things in the past but these leaders are confident enough to innovate and sometimes being even risk takers.

Example :Mother Teresa is an example of an initiating leader, She initiated service and human touch for all destitutes and homeless people in a developing country leaving her developed country behind. She was the first one to start the service for homeless people suffering with leprosy, in some cases where the family members turned their face from them. Mother Teresa gave them love, affection and respect apart from providing food, shelter and medical treatment with a dignified life.

- **System Leaders**

These leaders are very smart, in place of changing the whole system and innovating something new, they accept the existing system and bring changes gradually. This fetches least resistance and people get an improvised structure to work upon. They take no credit for these changes and invest their time and energy in overhauling the whole system.

Example : How can we forget former DG of Punjab Police - **KPS Gill, IPS** who did wonders in fighting and eliminating militancy from Punjab. Instead of changing the system, he adopted the consideration approach by bringing result oriented changes in the existing system and got tremendous success.

- **People's Leaders**

These leaders are people's representatives and they take care of their followers. Their main aim is to help and support their followers in achieving their goals and keep the welfare of their followers as the top priority. Some people argue that these leaders may neglect work or production output but I think the welfare of followers can be taken care of only if the system is supported and positive output is taken care of.

Example :Baba Ramdev and Anna Hazare showed courage to achieve success leading millions and billions of people. They led people for a corruption free India and bringing an effective Lokpal bill. They involved and gathered people from all sects of society to support the cause of a corruption less India.

- **Work / Output Oriented Leaders**

These leaders are successful in getting the work done at any cost. They finish projects at right time, plan their activities prioritising their work and achieve the goals of business within stipulated time limits. Some accuse them of being non-friendly and not people oriented but they can get the work done which in turn help their teams also.

Example :Sachin Tendulkar can be termed as a work oriented leader here. He believes in excelling to get the output for himself and for India. He could reach the Hall of fame with his dedication to get the results in our country's favour.

- **Development Oriented Leaders**

These leaders are dedicated to the cause of development, it may be of the company, country, society or people. They breath to develop and grow, not only for themselves but all others in the community. They are progressive and do not fizzle out easily.

Example : Who can be the best example then **Mr. Ratan Tata**, he is known for his welfare oriented development activities not only in Tata group but he has done a lot for the society also and has helped Indians in growing and facing the world with their chins up.

- **Authoritative Leaders**

These leaders command authority and know how to get the work done from others. They know how to manage people who do not wish to work, are lazy and shred responsibilities and mould them to be productive. These leaders are confident, self sufficient and knowledgeable enough to take drastic decisions, some may call them dictators but their authoritative style is not necessarily dictatorial in true sense.

Example : Who can forget the contributions of **Mr. T N Sheshen**, who was our Chief Election Commissioner and enjoyed his authority to bring landmark changes in our electoral system by making everyone understand their power to vote and managing the politicians well in their circle of authority.

- **Democratic Leaders / Team Leaders**

These leaders are team players. They avoid individual decision making and support their team members in their collective decision, listening, encouraging and taking everyone's opinion into consideration.

Example : **Mahender Singh Dhoni**, the Indian cricket team captain can be kept in this category. His democratic approach involved the veterans and new players together to win the 20 -20 World Cup, One Day Cricket World Cup and India maintained their top ranking in Test Cricket for a long time under his leadership.

- **Foresighted Leaders**

Foresighted leaders have a great foresight and they can foresee the future. They plan and execute in present for a successful tomorrow. They invest in the present to enjoy the fruit in future. They can predict effectively what people will be looking for in future.

Example : **Dr. K P Singh** of DLF is a Foresighted leader, when he was investing in a land in Gurgaon, no one could think that Delhi will not be able to accommodate the increasing need of business hubs and residential facilities and today, you name the MNC and you will find its office in Gurgaon.

> *Leaders lead from the front, they face the power of winds and the push of resistance but they never let the followers know that they are actually enjoying that.*

- **Flexible Leaders**

A very interesting question is 'What sort of leader should we become?'.Should we keep only one style in all situations or should we change as per requirements – the answer is to change as per the requirements, if the level of subordinates and specially if the situation demands we can be friendly, authoritative, democratic or supportive. It is sometimes not on the part of leader to adopt a particular leadership style but it majorly depends on the subordinates that what type of leader they should have. For an example you need to be quite authoritative for the followers who run away from their responsibilities and are malingers. For those who love to accept responsibilities, like work and are self-motivated the people oriented approach may be a good option.

Flexible leaders can adopt following 4 types of leadership styles depending on the requirements. I will try to explain this most important leadership style with the help of three examples consecutively. Where 1st example will be from personal life, 2nd will be from Corporate life and 3rd from History (from *GITA*, our sacred epic, which is an integral part of the generator of management – *Mahabharat*.)

A) Command Style

The leader decides what is to be done, who will do it and how it will be done. The leader only distributes the work among the subordinates. It is generally a one way direction and directive command is used (please note that directive command doesn't mean ordering or insulting tone). Generally this style can be adopted with the people with less mental maturity. They are just required to be given the directions like what to do and how to do a particular work. The logic and reasoning of the work to be done is not required to be explained and the subordinates understand that there should be some logic behind a certain type of command given by the leader.

Example 1 (Personal Life) : When the child is very small and is not able to understand the logic of a lot of things and asks everything from parents, like if he/ she has to go out to play, asking from mother becomes a regular phenomenon as the child is not able to take his own decisions. To such a question the mother may say – 'No, first finish the milk and then only go out to play'. The child will take the glass of milk, will finish it somehow and after asking from his / her mother only will go out to play. Please note that the child is not able to understand the logic of taking milk and is not able to take any decision and that is why asking his/her mother for her permission to go out as the child believes whatever parents are saying, are saying for good.

Example 2 (Corporate Life) : If you ask your driver to take a right turn whereas your office is towards the left side, do you think he will ask the reason?, No, he will just take a right turn presuming that you may be having a meeting with someone or you may be going to have breakfast with someone. Similarly if you ask your office boy for 3 cups of tea, do you think he will inquire, why 3 cups are required when you are sitting all alone? He will presume that someone is coming to have tea with you or you take more tea to cure headaches.

B) Explanation Style

In this style the leader has to explain the whole situation before assigning the task to the subordinates. This style can be adopted with the people having moderate level of mental maturity and with those who can understand the reasons explained by the leader. Once the subordinates understand the reason and logic of the work to be done, they do it with full enthusiasm and vigour. The behaviour of the leader in this case is less directive and more explanatory.

Example 1 (Personal Life) :A teenager, in place of 'asking' will 'inform' his / her mother that he/she is going out with friends. Now if the mother says no and asks him / her to take the milk first, teenager will start asking the logic, why should he/she take the milk, when his mother is taking the tea? What are the advantages of milk and what will happen if milk is not taken etc. Now the mother has to adopt the explanatory style to explain the logic first, the logic of milk in this case. Once she explains the idea of milk, its usefulness for teenager's body and how milk will help him/her in making the mind stronger to finish the homework fast and how it will make the body strong to be able to do more of physical activities and sports, The teenager will understand the explanation first and then only will take the milk.

Example 2 (Corporate Life) :If you ask your junior managers to increase the sales by 5%, it will never happen if you ask it without giving any logic. Here also you need to adopt the explanation style by explaining them that this 5% increase in sales will not only increase the revenue for the company but will also pave the path for their increments and promotions. After this 'explanation' only the sale can be increased.

C) *Cooperation Style*

The leader in this style of leadership is very cooperative and let the decision be taken by the subordinates, of course his guidance and support is there to make sure that the decision taken by them is right and fruitful. This style can be adopted with the subordinates who are self motivated, willing to work on their own, take decisions, are intelligent, having very good subject knowledge and can perform with little help and support from the leader.

Example 1 (Personal Life) : When the teenagers grow up as adults, they take their own decisions and you just need to cooperate them in taking the ideal decision (details are covered in the chapter of Decision Making), of course you can play the role of Devil's Advocate to cooperate only in helping them to take the decision of their choice.

Example 2 (Corporate Life) : To your senior managers, you do not give command or explain anything as they are experienced and specialists in their fields, you take their 'cooperation' in achieving a target or goal and also cooperate them in achieving the milestones for the company.

D) Support Style

The leader in this style has to guide or dictate nothing as the subordinates are experts in their area of expertise. The leader has to just make sure that only the outside support is provided to them so that they can perform well.

Example 1 (Personal Life) : For adult decision making, only outside support is required. When you have challenges in life, generally you do not ask for small helps from others, only a little support solves the issues. For an example the decision of a particular school or profession for someone's kids, you can surely give your views but as parents know about the subject matter better than you so they only take their own decisions.

Example 2 (Corporate Life) : With head of the departments and with senior managers, the command, explanation or cooperation style just does not work. You need to support them to plan for the growth of their departments and putting up execution polities as desired strategically. A lot of guidance can be termed as interference in their work and they need to be just supported within the parameters of guiding principles of the organisation.

Now we will discuss about our third example on leadership which is from Gita, we will study here Lord Krishna as a leader and will understand how he could achieve some impossible tasks with his amazing leadership styles.

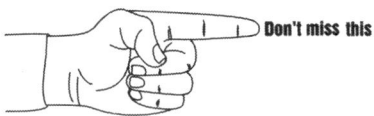 Don't miss this

Krishna as a Flexible Leader

Let us study Lord Krishna as a successful flexible leader. How he changed his leadership style as per different situations will be the matter of study for us. His strategies and his approach as per different situations in Mahabharat makes him one of the most successful leaders and managers the world has ever seen.

When he dealt with Pandavas (5 brothers) he flexibly changed his style of leadership to suit their requirements. The results were amazing and without dynamism in flexible approach, probably it was not practically possible. Studying one by one how he managed, guided and lead different Pandavas is an amazing case study in itself. Let me remind you again that we are studying Lord Krishna as a leader and manager and not as a God at present for the sake of our understanding of flexible approach of leadership.

Commanding Bhima as per Requirements

Bhima was the second eldest Pandava after Yudhishter and had a huge built. Being a wrestler he was physically stronger of them all but his level of mental maturity was not comparable with other Pandavas. Krishna managed him like a kid only and commanded him for his actions, even if he had to fight with someone, he used to ask Lord Krishna first (his dialogue – 'Bhratashri, Yadi Aap Kahen To Mein Eska Sar Phor Dun' (Brother, if you say, should I smash his head) became very famous during Mahabharat days in India, Krishna dealt with him in 'Command Style'

and commanded him whenever he wanted Bhima to fight or kill someone – the same happened in case of Keechuk elimination and the same with Jarasangha. When Bhima defeated Jarasangha, he did not die. Bhima looked towards Krishna, who picked up a straw, tore it into two pieces and threw it away. Bhima got the command and did the same with Jarasangha. But Jarasangha's body kept joining again and again. Bhima looked towards Krishna for further command, this time Krishna picked up a straw, tore it into two pieces and threw them in opposite directions (as he knew that Jarasangha had this blessing). Bhima did the same and after tearing Jarasandha, threw him in opposite directions and he could not join back as his blessing was for joining in same direction and not in opposite direction. When Krishna threw the torn straw in cross directions, Bhima never questioned Krishna as he was accepted as the undisputed leader and unchallenged manager of that time.

Explaining Arjun to Rewrite the History

The commanding style of leadership did not work with Arjun and he dropped his weapons in the battlefield before the battle and refused to fight against his grandfather he loved the most – Bhishma. He made it clear to Krishna that he cannot kill his Guru – Drona and his cousins - Kauravas, even if they were towards the opposite side and were facing him in the battlefield.

Lord Krishna immediately adopted 'Explanation Style' of leadership and explained the whole concept of Karma (duty) and Dharma (Religion), for effectiveness. Krishna played the role of a salesman who is committed to his cause to sell his idea, he dedicatedly explained the whole detail with a positive outlook to achieve the unexpected which changed the history. When the battle of Mahabharat (which continued for 18 days) started, for first 12 days Kauravs under the able leadership of Bhishma Pitamah, who was the commander of Kauravas, kept on defeating Pandavas and kept on advancing as no one could face Bhishma because he was blessed to die wishfully. When Pandavas discussed this challenge with Lord Krishna (as we corporate managers discuss in our board meetings with our CEO) he smiled (a unique quality of a successful manager to smile in difficult situations too) and explained that Pandavas should not be fearful with the fact that Bhishma has been blessed with wishful death as it doesn't mean that he will keep on living forever. Krishna advised all Pandavas to concentrate on the weakness of their opponents (here specially in case of Bhishma Pitamah) and guided them to hit upon such weaknesses (this is what we do today even with our corporate competitors. We look towards their product weakness and hit on that point to make our product or service successful).

It was observed that Bhishma Pitamah has got the ability to cut any arrow coming towards him and his weakness was really difficult (only difficult and not impossible) to find. However here Bhishma's principles come in his way, his principle was not to fight with any women, minor, unarmed or handicapped person. Pandavas thought of bringing a women in front of Arjun so that they can stop the arrows of Bhishma Pitamah towards him but as it was not possible to bring a woman to the battlefield so they arranged for an eunuch – Shikhandi and placed him in front of Arjun. Now Bhishma could not shoot arrows towards Arjun as Shikhandi was shielding him. The competent manager (Krishna) after doing the SWOT (strengths, weaknesses, opportunities and threats) analysis told the executive (Arjun) to execute (shoot his arrows) towards Bhishma with a precision to pierce through his body to make him immovable, Krishna was knowing that if someone cannot move, he cannot remain the commander of the forces.

Now the working executive (Arjun) picked up his bow and arrows and tighten the string of his bow again for final execution and pulled the string to check its strength. The saying is that the sound of this string spread the message of a new history which was about to be written in this battlefield of Kurushetra. Now Arjun started shooting his arrows towards Bhishma and they pierced through his body. He fell down on the ground and was forced to give the reins as the commander of Kauravs to Guru Dron.

Taking Cooperation from Yudhishter as a Strategy

Now if one problem was solved another one came up, in place of Bhishma, Guru Dronacharya became the Commander of Kaurav forces. Guru Dron who was so committed to make Arjuna as the best archer of the world that he demanded the right hand thumb from Eklavya, was now facing him only in battlefield, see the destiny the best Guru of the world was facing the best archer of the world.

Obviously Arjuna was not having any answer to the sharp arrows of Guru Dron and it seemed impossible for Arjuna to defeat Guru Dron. Again Pandavas had a meeting with Krishna and they thought of hitting Guru Dron on his weakness. It was established that Guru Dron was highly emotional and he will not fight if the news of the death of his son – Ashwatthama is given to him. Krishna asked Pandavas to eliminate Ashwatthama and spread the news of his death, to which they objected and told Krishna that it is impossible to eliminate Ashwatthama as he is a great warrior and is blessed to live long.

Krishna told them to listen to him carefully (for more details on listening skills, refer the chapter of communication), he said 'I have told you to eliminate Ashwatthama and not necessarily Guru Dron's son Ashwatthama, there is an elephant with the same name Ashwatthma, you can kill that elephant and spread the word that Ashwatthama has died. (interesting to know that Krishna was knowing even the names of the animals in battlefield, how many of our managers know all employees with their first name in companies).

Pandavas did the same, they located the elephant Ashwatthama and killed him and spread the word around. Guru Dron could not believe, how someone can kill his son who is a great warrior. He refused to believe the news, now it was Krishna's task to make sure that Guru Dron listens to them and believes them. If a normal person would have been handling this situation, he would have lost the hope but Krishna thought of a trick and expected Yudhishter to say that Ashwatthama has died because Yudhishter was the man of principles, he always spoke the truth, his words were believed truthful always by everyone including Guru Dron.

Now this task of getting it out from Yudhishter seemed to be impossible, Krishna could not give the 'command' and it was not possible to 'explain' this to Yudhishter, so Lord Krishna adopted the 'Cooperation Style' and asked Yudhishter to 'Cooperate' by saying the truth only but with voice modulation.

Krishna asked Yudhishter to say loudly – "Ashwatthama has died – 'human or elephant', I don't know", and to remember to do the voice modulation and utter the words 'human or elephant', I don't know" very slowly so that it does not reach Guru Dron. Yudhishter did the same but just to make it doubly sure that the words 'human or elephant' does not reach Guru Dron, as soon as Yudhishter said "Ashwatthama has died..." (Krishna blew a 'Shankh'), so the only words reached to Guru Drona were - "Ashwatthama has died". Guru Dron was shocked and his heart broke, he dropped his weapons with few questions in his mind – 'why should I fight, for whom, who will see me as victorious, who will call me victorious, for what I came here to win or to lose, the loss was very big, losing his own son (he thought), there is no logic of fighting this battle anymore, my son is gone – my world is finished'.

Drupada's son Dhristadyumna took this opportunity and beheaded the unarmed Drona who was sitting for meditation. This was the end of a great Guru — Guru Dronacharya.

Supporting Nakul and Sahdev in Decision Making

Nakul and Sahdev were very intelligent for the work they were assigned to. They were not required to be guided by Krishna on almost every step the way he guided Arjuna and Bhima or sometimes even Yudhishter.

Both Nakul and Sahdev knew what they need to do and whom they need to fight. They had never faced warriors like Duryodhan or Karna, that is why Krishna adopted 'Support Style' in place of commanding, explaining or Cooperation.

Impossible was made possible by Krishna with his charisma. He adopted different styles of leaderships with different Pandavas as per different requirements and made sure that desired outcome was achieved. He had to play different roles like that of a leader, friend, guide, counsellor, supporter and the most interesting one was as the charioteer of Arjun and never thought that becoming a charioteer is below his level or stature in society (can we all managers pick up any job like that if time requires? Do we not think of our 'status' in company and society before performing any such job?)

It is not necessary that you need to choose and become only one of the above type of leaders. You can choose to be a combination of the best styles suited to you.

How Can You Become A Leader

Some people hate theories and believe only in the practical aspects of life. They claim to have read many theories which sometimes teach them 'what' but not 'how'. My opinion is that theories are the foundation stones of the building of your success, even if they are not visible but they are very important for a strong base. However the 'how' alongwith 'what' is equally important. There are some theories which do not help because they are read with the motive of passing examinations only and not with the aim of understanding and implementing in day to day life. Here are some practical ways extracted from best of the leadership theories which will help you in becoming an effective Leader.

A. *By Accepting Leadership Challenges*

You need to stand up and claim you can lead otherwise how others will come to know about you and your confidence. They are never going to appoint you as a leader without you yourself taking a claim for that. You need to accept the challenge, you need to be ready to accept defeat sometimes and need to lose some battles to win the war. Until you face the challenge and take head on collusion with challenges and problems, how can you defeat the hiccups in the path of becoming a great leader. Be a volunteer to be a leader.

B. *By Believing in Your Abilities*

Identify and sharpen your abilities, understand and improve on your weaknesses and practise continuously to believe in your abilities. The success will be yours for sure. If you do not believe that you possess abilities to win, you need to change – either your abilities or your beliefs. Dedicated chapters on abilities required for success is given in this book for detailed study.

C. By Learning New Traits

Your present abilities are never enough to be a great leader, learn new abilities, inculcate new positive and result oriented habits (for details refer to the chapter on Habits), practice sincerely and do not leave consistency and perseverance. You will be amazed with unexpected positive results.

D. By Accepting A Different (or Difficult) Task

People generally pick up the easiest path to success, the different or difficult challenges are untouched and unexplored. Running away from difficulties can take you away from possible solutions too. A habit of accepting challenges, solving them as a way of life and not considering them as a part time activity will surely help you out in becoming a successful leader.

E. By Setting Higher Goals

Imagine a football match without goal posts. Our life will be such a game without any goals. Leaders not only set their goals but motivate and encourage others also to achieve these. Setting goals is a very important step in the journey of your success, the goal should not be very big that you start believing that you cannot achieve it so you even stop trying or feel demotivated and it should not be too small that you achieve it quite easily and that is why there is no motivation to work hard.

F. By Communicating Effectively

What you think and believe should be conveyed with effective communication and body language? Your words can create a magic, picking up right words for right people at the right time is the magic you can learn by listening to successful leaders and you can sharpen this ability with practice.

G. By Behaving Differently (Out of Ordinary)

First observe how ordinary people behave. You need to behave just opposite. Say thanks to someone doing something for you even if it is his / her duty (for an example even say thanks to a lift operator who operated for you even if it is his duty). Feel sorry, offer help, praise others and show interest in other people and their work, your different (better and appreciated) behaviour will help you out in becoming a successful leader.

> *You need to start believing that you can become a leader, the world will believe you were born that way.*

H. By Bringing Change

Accepting the given is not the leader's trait. Leaders bring changes and more importantly – positive changes. They change the people around them and then the world changes as per their will and wish, bringing change is the toughest job which only successful leaders can do.

When we occupy a high position in an organisation, do we understand the pain of people working with or under us. Do we understand their problems? Do we understand them entering into their shoes? Do we empathise with them? Do we realise from what condition they are going through, what are their needs and how they should be treated?

In some organisations, it has been noticed that if somebody is coming late, managers punish them without even thinking that they are leaving late also, if somebody is spending the minimum hours required in office then late reporting is out of question. It should be the output and not the timings in office which you should concentrate on as we are paying them for output and not the time spent in office. If the discipline of reporting at the right time in the morning is implemented, it should be implemented in the evening hours also, it has been observed that some managers give a lot of attention in reporting timings in morning but forget to implement the same in the evening. The research says that employees love and respect the bosses who ask them to leave at the right time. This way the work-life balance is also maintained and motivation of employees is also high.

> *Excuses are worse than even lies. In lies, you cheat others but in an excuse you cheat your own self.*

Let me share a story of a leader of his field – a lawyer who was known for his leadership skills.

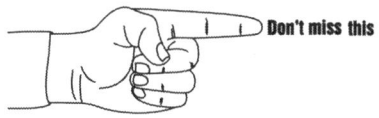
Don't miss this

The Cigars

This intelligent leader, who was a lawyer bought a pack of very rare and precious cigars and got these insured for a big sum by paying heavy premium. One day in a special party he opened the packet of his rare cigars and enjoyed the smoke with his friends. Soon he realised that he has turned all his rare cigars into ash, he decided to claim it from the insurance company but the insurance company refused to pay the claim because the lawyer himself lit the cigars. The lawyer filed a law suit in the court and

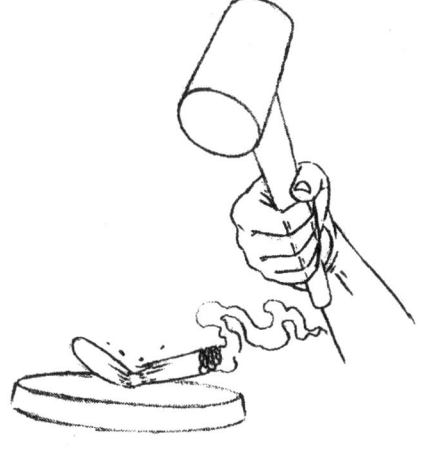

contested that he was indemnified for any type of loss by fire to his property and because he has lost his cigars to fire and he has paid the premium so he should be given the insurance claim. His trick worked and he won the case and got a huge sum of money.

The insurance company, after paying for the loss of cigars felt cheated and decided to sue the lawyer for intimidating the case and criminal conspiracy by exposing his property to fire himself. They filed a writ in the court by saying that if the loss would have been caused by natural fire, they were responsible for indemnification but in this case where the insurer himself has caused the fire and did not take any legitimate precaution or action to stop and save his property from fire, rather enjoyed the smoke out of it, does not deserve the claim and not only they should get the claim back but the lawyer should be punished for criminal conspiracy and ditching the insurance company to make money.

The company won the case this time... who was the leader in the story – the lawyer (or liar) or the insurance company.

Management Lesson

A little bird was flying south for the winter. It was so cold, the bird froze and fell to the ground in a large field.

While it was lying there, a cow came by and dropped some dung on it.

As the frozen bird lay there in the pile of cow dung, it began to realise how warm it was.

The dung was actually thawing him out! He lay there all warm and happy and soon began to sing for joy.

A passing cat heard the bird singing and came to investigate.

Following the sound, the cat discovered the bird under the pile of cow dung and promptly dug him out and ate him!

Learnings from the Lesson:
Not everyone who drops shit on you is your enemy
Not everyone who gets you out of shit is your friend.
And when you're in deep shit, keep your mouth shut!

I cried for normal shoes, until I saw somebody wearing Nike.

6

DECIDE NOT TO PERISH

(The Learning of What and How)

Right Decision is not Yes and No. It is Yes and Go...

Decide not to Perish 129

One of the most critical ability one must have to be successful is to decide, so that we do not perish. What is decision making and how decisions are taken are important points to learn and understand, let us start with the help of an example to understand it in true sense.

I am going to give you a situation and you need to take the decision, please be ready with your pen / pencil. As soon as you take the decision, write it on a space provided in this book, later we will discuss in details about the pros and cons and rights and wrongs of decision making.

A Very Important Question to Answer Quickly...

Just imagine that you are going somewhere on feet and crossing two railway tracks, one is a dead track where trains never come and go and another one is a live track where trains keep on running. You observed that there is a child playing on the dead track and there are 5 children playing on live track, suddenly you saw train coming on the live track very fast  and these 5 children playing on live track are totally ignorant of this fast approaching train. If you do not take any action, the train will run over 5 children playing on this track. You are not having any other option but to change the lever of the track to save the life of 5 children, and by changing the level you can put the fast running train onto dead track.

The question is, will you change the track of the train to save the life of 5 children or not.

Write down, Yes or No, here only..............Yes / No.......................

Most of people will say Yes, they will change the track of the train to save the life of 5 children playing on the live railway track and let one child die in this change who was playing on the dead track, but this is not the right answer. The right answer is No, you should not change the track of the train, you must be thinking why, if you do not change the track those 5 children playing on the live railway track may die, read the following lines to understand the reason of right answer - No.

You have thought about the 5 children only, have you thought about the 1500 people and many innocent children travelling in the train. What will happen to them if you change the track of the train, the train with all innocent passengers will go on the dead track, where trains never come and go, very obviously it is not to be used as it is not safe. The train on such a dead track will meet with an accident for sure and many people will die, for no fault of theirs they will be punished.

Second point here is that neither you are working for the railways, nor you are authorised to touch anything such as a lever to change the track of the train. It is a big decision and only railway authorities can do that, how can you think that you deserve to take the decision and you take it just because you cannot do any other thing to save those 5 children, whose parents are even not bothered about them and have left them to even play on railway tracks. Just a small check, can you allow your kids to play on railway tracks?

$$\left\{ \text{\textit{Last resorts are not decisions, the art of generating and picking up alternatives is a decision}} \right\}$$

Have you understood that your decision of saying 'Yes' was not right and it was an *emotional decision,* emotionally you could only think of those 5 children and not many children and people travelling in the train.

Some of you must have written 'No' very good - well done, you did not come in the emotional trap but what is the guaranty that you will not fall in other traps always while making decisions in your life and will always take *ideal decisions.*

I am sure the point is loud and clear that taking decision is not that easy, before we proceed further let us understand:

What is a Decision?

A decision may a defined as a choice made from available alternatives. But do you really think that the present alternatives are the only alternatives available or creativity can play a critical role?

The decisions are taken after considering all pros and cons. The pros and cons are the outcomes of the battle of 'Head' and 'Heart'. We choose some alternatives only with the help of our head and some only with the help of our heart, whereas the best decision can be taken on the basis of **Balance Theory** which suggests us the balanced way of decision-making using the head and the heart equally.

One of my most respected mentors, Prof. (Col.) P. S. Bajaj, Former Chairman – Institute of Management Technology – who not only taught me management but also motivated me to write this book has given an unmatched Decision Making Matrix, with different types of decisions taken either by head or by heart or by a combination of both head and heart. Let us see the details:

DECISION MAKING MATRIX

Acceptability (Heart)	Low (Quality of Decisions - Head)	High (Quality of Decisions - Head)
High	Group Decisions/ Emotional Decisions (III)	Ideal Decisions (IV)
Low	Flip of Coin or Roll of Dice Decisions (I)	Expert's Decisions (II)

Before we proceed further we need to understand that the decisions taken by head are the decisions which are good in quality and the decision taken by heart are easily accepted by others as the group connects with heart first.

Quadrant : I : Flip of Coin or Roll of Dice Decisions

In some cases decisions are taken by using lesser head and lesser heart and both the acceptability and the quality of the decision is very poor. If there are two things to choose from, flipping the coin to chose one alternative and if there are more than two choices, rolling the dice (with which we play Ludo) to get the answer without using head or heart will never produce best results. Rather it shows and proves that people not having the capacity to take decisions or not willing to use their head and heart for decision making take these types of decisions, which are not at all suitable for corporate of personal life decisions.

Example:-

The decision of having a soft drink brand is not a decision where people have to use their head or heart, whatever is available generally becomes the choice and that is why this is a flip of coin decision. On a Sunday, when you are sitting idle and doing nothing the decision of going to either a mall or for a movie is generally taken with a flip of coin. If there are more number of movies in the cinema, the choice of movie keeping in mind the time slots suitable for you sometimes becomes a decision of role of dice, for whichever movie you get the tickets and whichever is running in next few minutes becomes your choice of movie.

Quadrant : II : Expert's Decisions

These decisions are generally taken by experts (doctors, lawyers, engineers, CAs, MBAs, teachers, professors and professionals, etc.) who most of the times use only Head and not the Heart when it comes to their area of expertise in taking decisions. These decisions are no doubt very high in quality but are quite low in acceptability.

Example:-

A young boy of 10 years was crossing the road when a car knocked him down. He was rushed to a doctor (expert), who examined the injured boy and advised to dissect the crushed leg. The boy and his parents both cried a lot and requested the doctor to rethink his decision as this would make the boy handicap for rest of his life, but in vain. The leg was required to be cut to save his life; this was an expert decision where heart did not play any role or probably little role. The boy in the state of anaesthesia mumbled 'Daddy, I will join Army that is why I run regularly to keep myself fit and healthy, you don't worry I will fulfill your dream'. These statements were of no interest to the expert (Doctor) as he was busy in arranging for the tools in the operation theatre for the operation. This is a typical example of 'expert decision' where the mind plays a vital role and the heart the least.

Quadrant: III: Group Decisions or Emotional Decisions

On a lighter side, if you want to avoid any responsibility in future for your decisions, let a group take a decision for you, where everybody is involved in decision making but nobody can be blamed for any mess-up in future. Emotional decisions are generally taken by groups (individuals also take emotional decisions) and are quite high in acceptability but are low as far as the quality of decision is concerned. A lot of heart (feelings) is used and very less of head is used as the group psychology connects with heart with each other.

Example:-

When terrorists hijacked one of our IC 814 on 24th December 1999 and took it to Kandhar (Afghanistan), what type of decision was taken by the relatives of passengers. They took an emotional decision and did everything possible to put pressure on Indian Government to release the jailed terrorists. Was this decision in the favour of the Nation, was the question raised by masses? was this decision taken by heart and not by head ? Although we were able to save the life of around 172 people but the terrorists released in turn killed thousands later. They conspired against India and attacked on Parliament House (On 13th December 2001) in Delhi. They did a (26/11) attack in various parts of Mumbai including two 5 star hotels and attacked the American Cultural Centre in Kolkata on 22 January 2002. All these attacks were masterminded by the released terrorists from Indian jails.

What do you think? Was it a right decision? What would have been your decision if your parents or children had been kidnapped like this?

Quadrant : IV : Ideal Decisions

An ideal decision is considered to be the best, where both the head and heart are used to its maximum potential. These types of decisions are not only high in quality but are very good in acceptability too. Our aim should be to take ideal decisions in most of the cases, a perfect combination of utilisation of both head and heart is though not that easy but this way we not only look towards the quality and output of the decision but also ensure that it is accepted by everyone without any shadow of doubt.

> *Ideal decision is a balancing act like walking on a rope, you need to balance your head and heart equally to be successful.*

Before you expect me to explain how the ideal decisions are taken, let me share a small story with you all :

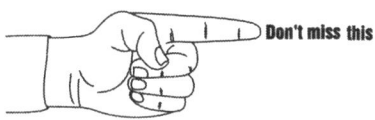 Don't miss this

First You Practise than You Preach

Meeta (a caring mother) took her son to a priest and told him that her son is a sugar crazy and takes as much as 20 spoons of sugar almost every day and she is tense about his health. She requested the priest to preach the son so that he should not take a lot of sugar.

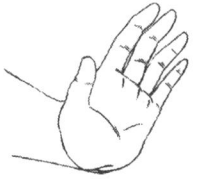

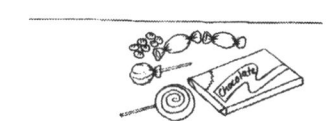

The priest requested her to come back after one week.

Meeta visited the priest after one week, changing two trains, one bus and then a rickshaw under the sun, quite tired. She reminded the priest about her request. The priest called Meeta's son and said- "Aati Sarvatra Varjayet" (Sanskrit) (English Translation : Excess of Everything is Bad). The priest explained the child how excess sugar can harm his body and can spoil his teeth too.

The child understood and promised not to take excessive sugar and left. Meeta was quite surprised, for such a small preaching why did the priest call her after a week, he would have said the same last time only as it just took him 5 minutes in explaining the child. Why she had to come all over again spending a considerable time and money on travel. She could not resist herself and asked the same from the priest.

The priest smiled and confessed that he could not preach the child that day as he himself was quite crazy about sugar and sweets. He wanted to practise the same control on himself first before preaching it to others. He asked Meeta how he can expect others to do which he himself can't, so he practised the control on sweets for a week on himself, mastered the art of control on sweets and then only he became eligible to preach others on the same. Meeta understood the greatness of the priest, thanked him and left happily.

That is why the saying – First You Practise than You Preach.

As a matter of fact I know what all are the ingredients required to make an awesome cake but I cannot teach you how to prepare a cake. You need a specialized pastry chef to let you know this with his skills to make an awesome cake, similarly I know the ingredients to take an ideal decision (like involvement of your head, heart and balance of both) but cannot tell you how to take ideal decisions. I am still a learner and the day I learn, I will be able to let others know 'how' to take the ideal decisions.

As far as the question of capabilities to take ideal decisions is concerned, let me tell you that all of us are suffering with **Hanuman Syndrome,** which means we have all the powers with us but we are not aware of them as *Lord Hanuman* was not knowing about his powers and *'Jamwant'* told them about the powers he possessed. *Jamwant* told him that he can fly in the air, he can jump the sea, can pick up mountains and fly. He can conquer all the challenges if he determines that.

We all are also suffering with Hanuman syndrome, we also possess many qualities and powers but either we do not know or we have forgotten them completely. In our life we need one *Jamwant* as a catalytic agent to be present to wake us up to tell us that what all powers do we possess. It may be the ability of ideal decision making, analytical analysis, creativity, social skills, planning abilities, execution capabilities or any other CSFs (Critical Success Factors).

How to Take Decisions Step by Step

The following are the details of how to take decisions step wise. These will help you out in learning the process gradually to practise and to make it a productive habit (please refer to the chapter of habits for more details).

• Understand the Challenge

Once the challenge is clear, you can make your plans accordingly. Well begin is half done. Understanding of the challenge as a first step will put you on the right track for the ideal decisions. We need to define what is the challenge in such a manner so that no ambiguity is left.

• Pick up and Weight the Right Criteria

There may be different criteria to take decision but you need to match the best suited criteria for the best of the results, there is no logic of taking the criteria which is not practically possible or is very costly, although the outcome counts but the economies and time factor are the important aspects in picking up the right criteria.

> *When we are ready to face the challenges, the size of the challenge reduces and the gravity vanishes.*

• Generate the Alternatives

The most challenging step in decision making is the generation of alternatives. You will never get enough alternatives in life, you need to generate it, produce it or source it with your abilities, with your creativity, with your education and with your experience, if you find yourself not fully competent for this step take someone's help who is more matured and more experienced. Once you understand how to generate alternatives, there will be no challenges which you find difficult to face.

No one came from London to invite Gandhi to do his barristership from England. No one told Subhash Chandra Bose that different counties will help him if he raises 'Indian National Army'. No one came to invite Amitabh Bacchan to give a role in the movies. All these men generated alternatives and fought their battle to be successful.

• Picking Up The Most Suitable Alternative For Best Results

Result Orientation is something all your seniors will be looking towards. You would love to invest your time and effort in positive and result oriented activities and actions so that you can pick up the most suitable alternative which can produce the best results. If you feel that you are working hard but not getting the results, change your alternative and pick the most suitable one for 'Result Orientation'.

Most of the decisions are taken keeping in mind the outcome or the maximum payoff from the decision. This type of decision-making is also known as rational decision making.

Role of Devil's Advocate

The decision making exercise in any group cannot be successful until and unless a *Devil's Advocate* is present in the group. This is a very positive term unlike it sounds as the devil's advocate is the person who questions the practicality of the decision to ensure that the decision taken is absolutely right and useful. The devil's advocate always asks, how, why, when, where and by whom to assure that the decision is taken in right prospective and is fruitful.

Types of Decisions

Programmed and Non Programmed Decisions

Keeping in view the occurrence of the problems, the decisions can be divided into programmed and non programmed decisions. Programmed decisions are the ones, which are programmed already and which you have taken earlier also. These can be taken in pre-empted situations whenever such situations arise. The non programmed are the ones, which are taken for the first time when some problem arises specially those challenges which you have not faced earlier. The value of a manager who is able to take the Non Programmed decisions is much more in any organization as comparatively non programmed decisions are tougher to take than the programmed decisions.

Individual and Group Decisions

Keeping in view the number of decision makers the decisions which are taken by individuals are the individual decisions and those which are taken by the groups are the group decisions. Here we will only talk about the group decisions because it has been proved beyond any shadow of doubt that ultimately the group decisions are better decisions (if these are ideal decisions then they are the best) in the long run.

Advantages of Group Decision Making

• **The Knowledge Ocean**

Individuals have got limited knowledge and they can plan and execute within the limits of their limited pool of knowledge only, in no case an individual can be smarter than a group of thinkers with greater pool of knowledge of different fields. When a group takes a decision, they collect the group knowledge first, churn it further and then extract the information from the data available to proceed further.

• **Multi Angled Point of Views**

The individuals cannot see all the aspects of a particular problem from all angles. A group of decision makers may be from different backgrounds with different experiences and can see the same thing from different point of views. For an example, a product will be seen from different angles like productivity and availability, the sales person will see the packaging, distribution and advertisements apart from publicity and the financer will look towards the price of the product comparing it with competitors. This gives the product the cutting edge in the market to be successful.

• **Training Platform for Learners**

Group decisions are a training platform for the learners who are yet learning how to take the group decisions and how to participate in the group decision exercises. In most of the cases the individual decision makers also learn from the group of specialised decision makers in a group. They learn to see different angles of the same aspect and learn to challenge their own decisions.

Disadvantages of Group Decision Making

No system in the world is perfect and is without flaws, there are some disadvantages of the group decision making, which are listed below:

• Time Consuming

The biggest problem with group decision making is that it is very time consuming, arranging meetings with all the decision makers is a challenging task and it takes a lot of precious time and effort on the part of the organiser.

• Group Pressure

Group pressure plays a negative role in group decision making and if your boss is also present in the group, it is always difficult for you to freely express your views specially if these are not matching with your boss. In our families also, sometimes in the presence of elders with a different set of thought process, it may be difficult for anyone to be vocal enough to put his / her point of view without any resistance.

• Majority Rules

If there are 10 people in the group and 3 are saying something and 7 are on other side, what do you think, which will be the final decision, the one suggested by 3 members or the one taken by 7 members. Obviously the final decision will be the one taken by 7 members but it doesn't mean that whatever is decided by 7 members is right, probably the one suggested by 3 may be ideal. Here the majority dominates the group and in place of ideal decisions, the decision taken by majority are final and binding to the group or organizations.

• Domination of Individual Interests

The individual biases of influential members in the group dominate the decisions and sometimes in place of 'Ideal' decision, the 'Beneficial' decisions for some influential members is taken. It may not be good for the organisation thought. (the decision of % of salary increase by HR Manager may fall in this category if his own salary is also linked directly with this %).

• Too Many Cooks Spoil the Both

Sometimes with different prospective or with a big number of contributors, the group is not able to reach on 'a' conclusion, where few will be in favour or something. Few will be opposing it and few will be sitting clueless or disinterested, for a better group decision making the group should not be too big and only the decision makers who will be 'answerable' in future should be invited to participate.

Management Lesson
Decision Making Should Become a Way of Life
Generally it is observed that when there is some problem or challenge and people are expected to take a decision, they procrastinate it by saying that they will see, they will ask someone's help, they will look for an alternative and they will try to overcome it soon but it never happens. The reason is that they take decision making ability as part time activity and not a way of life. Swami Vivekanand has said that if you have not faced any problem in a day, it means you are not going on the right path.

I am sure the right path is not easy, it is full of nails and tough challenges. When we wake up, we should be ready to face many challenges in the day, when the challenges come, we need to start executing our decisions. Expecting and accepting the challenges on daily basis and making decisions should be a way of life and certainly not a part time activity.

'If your father is a poor man, it is your fate, but if your father-in-law is a poor man, it is your fault, so take your decisions carefully.'

7

COMMUNICATE LIKE CRAZY

(The Effectiveness Tool)

Effective Communication is route map in the journey of success.

Communicate Like Crazy

A man asked a priest – 'Can I smoke while I pray', the priest got angry.

Man's friend asked the priest – 'Can I pray while smoking', Priest happily said "Yes"

It is not what you are asking; it is how you are asking.

The magic of positive outcome depends on the effective communication and it is the backbone of human life. All living beings communicate, may it be animals, birds or even insects but human beings are blessed with effective communication skills by God. These are most unique and effective communication skills we all are blessed with, the only point is how we all make use of this.

What is Communication?

Communication is the process of exchanging or sharing thoughts, which are shared and understood by others in the same meaning and context. The transference and understanding of meaning with or without words, with or without body language (gestures and posters) is also communication.

Before looking how human beings communicate, let us see some examples of other creatures and see how they communicate.

Have you observed in your homes that a single ant can call a group of ants if some eatables or some dead insect is available for them? It may be noted here that they spread a special type of chemical and with the fragrance all other ants come to know about the availability of the food.

The dance of the peacock is also another signal of attracting peahens. The whales whistle for other whales to let them know about the danger or food. The communication of bees is also world known. The communication of dogs without using a single world is quite effective and well known. They make you understand if they are friendly to you or hostile. They express all feelings very clearly and are able to communicate what they are thinking, what they are liking and what they intent to do, wagging their tails conveys friendliness and grumbling or showing teeth means anger.

Before we proceed further let us enjoy a story of a palmist and his son. You can observe how his son understood the value of communication and how he utilised these skills when required.

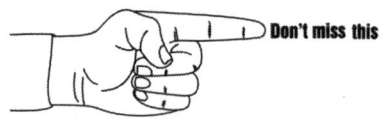

The Story of Two Palmists

A king named Manish Nand, wanted to know his future. He asked his ministers to call a palmist.

Bhatt, the most learned palmist was called and Manish Nand asked something about his future. Bhatt took Nand's palm in his hand and studied the lines for sometime and said : "Maharaj Nand, you will see all your near and dear ones dying in front of your eyes and you will have to cry for them all."

Manish Nand got very annoyed and ordered his soldiers to put Bhatt behind the bars. Bhatt was imprisoned for the words he uttered. The will of Manish Nand to know his future did not die with it and he again ordered his minister to call some good palmist. Another known palmist Sanjay was called to his palace. When Sanjay studied Nand's palm, he jumped with joy and said -"Maharaj Nand, enjoy, celebrate and distribute sweets – you have got a long life and you will enjoy all these facilities much more than anyone around you".

Manish Nand was amused to listen and immediately ordered his minister to reward Sanjay, who politely declined any prizes and gifts and requested the release of his father (Bhatt) who was in jail.

Nand was surprised to know that Bhatt is Sanjay's father. He asked Sanjay that how his father told him something which was annoying and how Sanjay told something which was pleasing. In answer Sanjay said, "What all my father said was absolutely right but the way he expressed was not right as he did not pick up the right words. I have said the same thing in different words and in a different way".

When Nand gave some attention on the gist of it he smiled because it was very clear that if he live longer he will be able to enjoy all these facilities much more than others but then he will have to see the death of all his near and dear ones too.

Nand praised Sanjay and awarded him with gifts and released his father too.

Moral of the story :

The effective communication is picking up the right and effective words at the right time and utilising them in the right manner. Effective communication can create a magic and unexpected can be expected in managing and motivating people.

Types of Communication

Verbal and Non-Verbal Communication

I am sure most of us understand verbal communication which is a blessing to human beings but equally effective is the non-verbal communication which includes your body language, gestures, postures and signals.

A manager is not required to use any words to show if he is happy or angry, his team can read from his body language the way he is behaving and conducting to know what the weather is.

Effective managers utilise the non-verbal communication in very effective manner, back patting a team member conveys a lot, clapping, giving positive support with thumbs up signal, smiling in difficult situations and shaking hands with team members can create a magic with the team members.

The Communication Barriers

Despite best efforts, sometimes the meaning is not communicated properly and it is because of a number of communication barriers, which hinder the proper flow of communication and distort the message. Here are some of the communication barriers, which can be mitigated if we take preventive steps in advance.

- **Perception** is a process by which individuals organise and interpret their sensory impressions in order to give meaning to their environment. It refers to the way the world looks, sounds, feels, tastes, or smells. Perception is one of the biggest barrier of communication because people are not able to communicate or understand the same meaning of words with similar words used by sender, for example when people make a statement, it is sometimes difficult for others to make out if it is a comment, compliment, praise, sarcastic remark or back-pat statement.

  Example: After seeing a project report the boss said, - 'I have never seen such a report in my life' – now can you guess the real meaning of this statement and can you guess the quality of the report as it can be a compliment or a sarcastic remark, either the report is very good or it is very bad.

  > *Sometimes without even uttering a word your message reaches successfully. It is not hard communication, it is heart communication*

- **Language and vocabulary** are the most obvious barriers because if you are not knowing that language well you can't make out what the other person is saying and what is to be done to give or receive the right signals. Even if you understand the language, sometimes you can't understand the words used by the speaker, even if your vocabulary is good, you can miss the real meaning of that particular word.

  Example : Sometimes, people confuse in being 'famous' and they land up becoming 'notorious', one Ox is Ox but two are oxen and there is no 'enter' in entrance, are some English words which can confuse someone.

- **Protectiveness** is a natural phenomenon where one is protective about himself / herself and about one's thoughts. Being over protective can conceal the exact information which directly or indirectly may harm the real meaning transference.
- **Presentation** is critical as it can change the whole meaning and effect of communication. If something good is presented in a bad manner or vice versa it can change the whole game. Just imagine with the best presentation of food and beverages how a 5 star hotel is able to charge exorbitant prices from the guests.
- **Sieving** is the process in which one keeps some information with him/herself and pass the rest after sieving as per choice, time, requirement and need of the hour. Sieving can be positive and negative and can be done in any manner, which generate the impact depending on the positive or negative sieving.

The Effectiveness of Communication

Some people communicate very effectively with positive and encouraging results. There have been people like Swami Vivekananda who have created the impression on all Americans during his address in the Chicago in late 19th century. His address of "My dear American Brothers and Sisters" impressed Americans in such a way that they still love and remember the preaching of Swamiji.

The communication of Sir Winston Churchill during the IInd World War is still remembered. The speeches of Pt. Jawahar Lal Nehru and Sardar Vallabh Bhai Patel cannot be overlooked during the time of independence of India. Atal Bihari Vajpai in modern age is considered to be a majestic orator. When these personalities spoke the effect was everlasting and remembered. What are the mantras to make the communication effective are given hereunder for your ready reference and practice.

The Mantras of Effective Communication

- **Adopt 'You' Attitude In Place of 'I' Attitude**

  This way you think how the other person is thinking and communicate other person's feelings and emotions standing in others shoes. In 'I' attitude it is sometimes difficult to connect with the person and it sounds a bit arrogant.

- **Two Way Communication** makes it effective when the source communicates, the target listens and when the target gives feedback the source listens, if the two way communication is done face to face, it is even more effective.

- **Match Actions with Words.** When you match your actions with your words and your words with actions, then only people respect you from their heart and listen to you carefully. If you do not match your actions with your words the credibility and value of your words is lost and the communication in that case cannot be effective.

- **Face-to-Face Communication.** Emphasis should be on face to face communication to ensure the correct and quick feedback. The other biggest advantage of face to face communication is to communicate through your body language and to observe the same of the opponent. The words may be false but the body language will speak the truth.

- **Responsibility for Communication.** Anybody and everybody who is communicating should be responsible for their words and communication. It is the tendency of normal people to add or delete something from their side and the perception, defensiveness, filtering, language and presentation also play a critical role. If people know that they can be held responsible for their communication, they pick up right words and communicate only when it is required, they only discuss the right and trusted data for decision making and do adopt careful approach in communication.

- **Message Should Be Shaped For Its Intended Audience.** The mental level, educational background, subject knowledge, the understanding of the particular subject matter and the level of interpretation of the target audience should be kept in mind at the time of communication so that they can understand the same meaning, which the communicator wants to communicate.

- **Treat Communication As An Ongoing Process.** The communication is an ongoing and continuous process and should be considered ongoing until and unless the point is properly communicated and clarified with correct feedback.

Sometimes people are confused in understanding the meaning of communication and that is why they always try to be good speakers and not good listeners. For effective and proper communication you not only need to be a good orator but a good listener too. Let us see some of the guidelines to be an effective listener.

How to be an Effective Listener

- **Accept the Speaker.** The first step to be an effective listener is to accept the speaker. Different people have different types of thinking; do not overload them with your ideas and understandings. If your role is to listen, just listen them and understand the subject matter.
- **Make Eye Contact.** With the speaker, in this case neither you nor the speaker is disturbed and the communication is complete. Your eye movement should be minimum and required as per the situation. If you move your eyes from the speaker, your attention also moves apart.
- **Exhibit Affirmations.** While playing the role of an effective listener, you have to exhibit affirmative head nods and appropriate facial expressions to make sure for the speaker that you are listening; you are interested and understanding whatever he or she is communicating.
- **Don't Confuse the Speaker.** Sometimes you will find that speaker is not having enough knowledge on the subject matter, it is still not advisable to jump immediately in between to correct him or to impress him or others with your

knowledge. Just pass the information in a very cool way at the right time and not during the flow of communication.

Today we don't need only good speakers, but good listeners too. If we have the qualities of a good listener, probably the struggles in the personal and corporate life will come to a negligible level.

Formal and Informal Communication

Formal communication is task related communication that follows the authority chain. This authority chain in a family may be – father, mother, children and then grandchildren. In the corporate sector, it may be chairman, directors, VPs, GMs, Managers, Staff Level personnel and the workers.

Informal communication is free from any authority chain to move in any direction, skip authority levels, and is as likely to satisfy group members' social needs, as it is to facilitate task accomplishments. There is no formal rule and regulation of communication and it may flow in any direction, any time, any day. **This is also known as grapevine** (because it is like the vine of the grapes where no order is visible and it can start and flourish from any direction and can lead to any direction as there is no perfect order or set pattern).

Grapevine may be very useful and it may also distort the whole communication badly. Although people use similar type of words and try to match the language but the meaning may completely change. To support this point here is the series of memos from a company, started by the managing director of a company and how and what is reaching to the marketing executives or the base level managers is given hereunder.

Grapevine Communication

MEMO

From: Managing Director   To: Vice President

"Tomorrow morning there will be a total eclipse of the sun at nine o'clock. This is something which we cannot see every day.

So let all employees line up outside, in their best clothes to watch it. To mark the occasion of this rare occurrence, I will personally explain the phenomenon to them. If it is raining we will not be able to see it very well and in that case the employees should assemble in the canteen."

Translated:

From: Vice President   To: General Manager

"By the order of the Managing Director, there will be a total eclipse of the sun at nine o'clock tomorrow morning. If it is raining we will not be able to see it in our best clothes, on the site. In this case the disappearance of the sun will be followed through in the canteen. This is something we cannot see happening everyday."

Translated

From: General Manager   To: Industry Manager

"By order of the Managing Director, we shall follow the disappearance of the sun in our best clothes, in the canteen at nine o' clock tomorrow morning. The Managing Director will tell us whether it is going to rain. This is something which we cannot see happen everyday."

Translated

From: Industry Manager   To: Location Head

"If it is raining in the canteen tomorrow morning, which is something that we cannot see happen everyday, the Managing Director in his best clothes, will disappear at nine o'clock."

Translated

From: Location Head   To: Marketing Executives

"Tomorrow morning at nine o' clock, the Managing Director will disappear without his clothes. It's a pity that we can't see this happen everyday"

Are you laughing, it is really worth a good laugh but the Grapevine Communication should not be taken negatively in all cases. Sometimes Grapevine communication is so important that you can use it to get your work done in a very effective manner. Just see how a manager – Vikas is utilising Grapevine Communication.

> *Grapevine communication is like a double edged sword, you need to be smart enough to get the double advantage rather than getting hurt.*

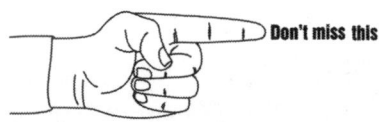
Don't miss this

Case Study of Vikas, A Smart Manager, Utilising Grapevine Communication

Vikas, a manager, got the information from his general manager that they are bound to cut 5% of the salary of the workers because of some adverse business circumstances. Vikas was expected to inform this to workers in such a manner that neither there should be any unpalatable reactions nor there should be any IR problem in the company.

Vikas knew both types of communications - the formal and the informal communication (i.e. Grapevine). He was very sure that if he utilises the formal type of communication (i.e. notice, mail, memo etc.). This news is going to be a fireball in the company so he decided to take the help of grapevine communication and spread the news with the help of some of his near and dear ones that due to some unavoidable reasons the upper management is cutting some salary of workers but Mr. Vikas with the help of the GM is trying his level best to avoid it, which almost seems impossible.

With this type of rumours (spread by Vikas knowingly) workers got the information of the adverse business conditions and they were mentally prepared to face the situation, but to avert it to the maximum possible extent they approached Vikas for clarification

Communicate Like Crazy 153

because it was not communicated through formal communication (notice, etc.).

Vikas was also prepared for that and welcomed the workers. They shouted anti management slogans and tried to put pressure on the management through Vikas. They also tried to emotionally blackmail Vikas by quoting their problems of high expenditure for their children's education, transportation and other problems in this tough time of high inflation.

Vikas welcomed them and asked to speak one by one and just listened to them patiently first. He calmed them down for sometime and when he observed that the workers have spoken from their side, he took the opportunity to speak and addressed them in the following manner.

"My dear brothers", (Appropriate salutation)

"I can understand your feelings right now (showing empathy). I know you all are facing a lot of hardship because of high prices and high cost of living (showing concern and sharing feelings). Being a salaried person I am also facing these challenges (showing them that he is in the same boat). When I heard this rumour (which he himself had spread), I went to the GM to clarify the facts. I knew our company is facing a lot of financial challenges and in this way the show can't be managed anymore to continue and if it is not solved the company may shut down (indirect threatening to shut down). The only solution left is to manage somehow with the lower cost and that is only possible, when we all extend a helping hand to our company in this tough time. I know you have always helped the company and we have always worked as a team. How can we run away from our responsibilities now? Let us join hands and help our company to help us in managing our family affairs in future. I just want to clarify one more fact that almost every company in the same trade has done so to survive because in this adverse situation almost all the companies have suffered badly. Let us contribute something to save it for the bright future and pray to God to empower all of us and to confer us with his blessings to face such a tough situation. To support my company I have decided to share 5 % of my salary, I am sure you will also help your company to help you out later"

All the workers understood the situation and promised to give the 5% happily.

> This was only possible with the help of the grapevine communication and if it would have been the formal communication like notice or memo to supervisors then company may have faced a strike or lockout situation because of rejection of the pay cut.

Let us solve a communication riddle...

First Situation

The boss is sitting in his office and eagerly waiting for one of his juniors who is carrying some important papers for the presentation for senior management. There is no information and no phone calls from his junior, why is he late?, where is he? and when is he reaching?. The telephone bell rings and the secretary picks up the phone and ensures that this was the same junior for whom the boss was eagerly waiting for. Secretary transfers the call to the boss, the boss yells, "Where are you bloody fool, come soon, otherwise you will have to face the music." The boss looked very angry and annoyed.

Second Situation

After sometime, again the bell goes, again the secretary picks up the phone and again she transfer the line to boss, again boss yells, "Where are you bloody fool, come soon, otherwise you will face the music." This time the boss was very happy and smiling.

Please analyse and describe how at second time the boss is happy, how can he be happy. He has used the same words in the same tone in the same pitch and he was so tense a few minutes back. All other employees who observed this were surprised, confused and did not believe that second time the boss used the same words but in a happy tone. Can you solve the riddle... please take some time to think and try to answer the reason of sudden change before reading the following paragraph.

Actually the second time it was the phone of one of the closest friends of the boss who was visiting here after many years and was calling from the airport whereas the boss was eagerly waiting for him. Now you can understand that the same words and the same tone may have different meanings.

The subordinate, who was late, got it as a bashing and the friend of the boss felt very happy because these words were used in such a situation where a friend was showing his eagerness to meet him.

Richness Level of Channels of Communication

The richest channel of communication was, is and will be the Face to Face communication because we are not only able to see and listen the person, we are able to see his/her body language, expressions, gestures and postures, we can see the reactions of our communication and facial expressions as a feedback, face to face it is difficult for someone to hide all the emotions, say if we are talking to someone and he/she is smiling and nodding the head gives us the feeling that person is interested in listening to us but is the person is looking towards the watch again and again, makes it clear that the person is not interested and looking to go now.

The following is the list of Channels of communication on richness scale wise :

- **Face to Face Communication** (is the richest channel of communication)
- **Video Conferencing** (this is not as rich as face to face because we are not able to see the complete body (language) and only face is visible, the person must be shaking his legs under the table in a video conferencing which means under confident sometimes)
- **Telephone** (not as rich as video conferencing as we are not able to see the person or his / her body language), with the help of the following example, it is easy to understand this point clearly :

Example:

Atul, a bank customer called at 9 am on phone banking to know his bank balance, the following communication took place :

Bank Operator : Good Morning Sir, ABC Bank, how can I help you?

Atul : Hi, I am Atul and my account no. is 7560XXXX897, I just wanted to know my bank balance.

Bank Operator : Thank you for calling Sir. Can you please hold for a minute (Atul heard her typing his account no. on her computer). I am sorry sir, our server is down, may I request you to call us in an hour's time, I apologise for the inconvenience.

Now what is your view about this communication? What do you think about the telephone operator? You just heard her and have not seen her, I am sure you will say, she is quite professional and courteous, she is helpful and felt sorry when she could not help the customer.

Now the real story : The operator's duty timings were from 9 am. As per the bank rule, she should have been on her desk by 8:55 am but she entered the office at 9 am only. As soon as she entered, she heard the phone bell and picked up Atul's call who wanted to know about his bank balance. Now to give Atul a feeling that she is typing his account number in computer, she started pressing some random keys (of computer which is not yet switched on) and misguided him that server is down and asked Atul to call after an hour.

Now what do you say about the richness of face to face and telephonic channel of communication.

- **E mails** (neither we are able to see the person not we can observe body language but it is still better than letters as we can put clip art pictures, colours, can change fonts, can attach power point presentations and can take the help of word art)
- **Memo / Letters** (these are not as rich as e-mails being just black and white, the maximum we can do is to underline and bold a few points).

Let us see an example of Communication.

A publisher while checking the final proof read the following line and could not understand the meaning of the sentence. Can you please explain the meaning of the following sentence?

The cow said the teacher is a useful animal.

At the time of printing the commas were missed out. The publisher's editor asked his assistant to put the commas in the text line to give it a meaning, the assistant placed a coma and now the sentence is printed as follows :

The cow said, the teacher is a useful animal.

The meaning is quite absurd, how a cow can speak and how the teacher can be an animal, useful or not, is a different issue altogether, the Publisher got annoyed and asked the assistant to put two comas this time at the right place.

Now when the commas are placed on the right places, the sentence looks like this :

The cow, said the teacher, is a useful animal.

Practical Use of Effective Communication

In many business schools and educational institutions, I have faced this question and thought of mentioning it here as the debate of theoretical and practical knowledge is always alive. If we are not able to convert our theoretical knowledge into practical aspects, there is no use of spending years and years of studies.

Here we will discuss about the practical use of effective communication and will see some practical techniques to ensure the desired positive outcome :

A) *How To Make Your Boss Listen To You*

Before making your boss listen to you, understand the boss. A boss is an authority in his office and all surroundings like his phone / blackberry, laptop, office interiors, files, charts, papers, books, high back chair, big table, plush office and everything present in his office reminds him again and again that he is the **boss**. If you want to communicate something to him, it will be comparatively easy to do it to your friend than to your boss, you obviously can't make your boss a friend but you can bring him to the same level. If you need to communicate something to your boss, request him to accompany you for a cup of tea/ coffee and invite him to your company cafeteria /or at any other cafe (where others should not disturb him and you).

Now when you two are sitting on a café table for a cup of coffee, he is sitting on a common café table (not on his authoritative table) on equal platform on similar type of chair in friendly atmosphere (away from his authoritative office where nothing is reminding him that he is a Boss) now this is the right atmosphere and situation to start your communication.

Always start your communication with a positive and lighter topics of interest and with the agreement of both parties. Later when you feel it is the right time to start effective communication (when the coffee has arrived and its fragrance and taste is going to make the atmosphere more soothing) ask his approval to share your 'feelings', you can share your feelings in a firm tone without saying something in a requesting or complaining tone. Share what your feelings are, share what you think 'should be', understanding his standing on different topics. In case of controversial topics, keep the words very crisp and prefix it with your 'feelings', if he is not accepting, you can take the words back by saying, these were just your feelings only. Now share what you want, ask him if you are asking for a lot or it is justified. Ask his views on your feelings and ask him to correct you if you are not on the right track, share what you want and see if he can help you, after listening to him, conclude this communication with a positive note with a thanks for his time, patient hearing and guidance.

B) How To Deal With Your Critics

The second critical question I have faced is – how to deal with your critics. Answering this in many business schools and to many working executives has given me the idea to put it in this book.

If you have a critic in your company, take it easy and take it positively first of all, your critics raise the standard of your work, thinking and performance. The second step you need to take is to identify the critic's strong and positive points and start praising him in front of others, keep on praising him almost every day for something (everyone of us is a package of good and bad points, if you concentrate well, you can find some faults with good people and some good points in bad people).

Now what will happen after about a week, your critic will feel good listening to his praises from different people in office and will try to make sure that you keep on doing it (who is not eager to listing to their praises) and he will be under pressure to keep this habit of yours to continue and to balance he will be left with no option but to stop your criticism and slowly start praising you in return. If at all he continues to criticise you even your boss and others will not give him any attention as they have observed you praising him. Even they can ask your critic – what type of person he is, someone praising him and you are criticising. Criticism cannot stand against praise for a minute and all his criticism will lose the ground, as a natural reaction, your praise for him will make your critic your friend and fan.

How To Make Communication Effective In Organisations

The magic of communication is not only for individuals, it can even change the fate of any organization. We just need to know some mantras for the effectiveness of communication in the organizations. Following are some mantras to make sure that every communication ultimately proves to be effective and yields positive desired results.

- **Complaint and Suggestion Boxes**

Just keeping complaint and suggestion boxes will not solve your problems if you do not give attention on what happens after someone puts something in those. Who opens it and what actions they take, where these are placed will also play a critical role in effectiveness as generally an employee feels hesitant to put something in open. Put them in rest rooms and see the amazing results, if the feedback is given to all those who are complaining and suggesting will reduce both complaints and suggestions (more suggestions means more people believe, you are not on the right track). Even if you are not able to work on their complaints or not able to implement these suggestions, the honest feedback will reduce 50% of the problems and will be the key to relieve the pressure from the 'pressure cooker' (unheard employee).

• Open Door Policy

People say that open door policy is not successful because ' **if you keep your door open, you AC will not be effective'.** Jokes apart, the open door policy is only successful if subordinates and juniors believe in your ability to handle the information and to take critical and ideal decisions. If after listing to some complaint from a worker either you do not take any action or overreact like you call and shout on your managers, you will fail miserably in the implementation of this policy as your managers will make the life of your workers hell if they enter your chamber. Open door policy is not for pointing fingers or finding faults with your managers, it is for the release of pressure from the 'pressure cooker'. Listing, getting facts, knowing why it is happening and understanding the psychology of your workers will make your 'open door' an effective 'open mind door' for your own and company's success.

• Exit Interviews

As a ceremony or as a routine if you conduct Exit Interviews, you are bound to fail. If you 'conduct' exit interviews 'formally' again you may not be successful. Only informal and friendly exit interviews are effective, never expect the outgoing employee to 'fill' any information in the 'forms' because it has been observed that employees are always hesitant in giving anything in black and white. Be friendly and extract information making use of your effective communication. You may get some very useful information to improve the organization.

On a lighter side, enjoy the following management lesson...

Management Lesson

A manager offered a lift to a secretary. She got in and crossed her legs, forcing her gown to reveal a leg. The manager nearly had an accident. After controlling the car, he stealthily slid his hand up her leg. The secretary said, "Sir, remember rule 10 of our organization?" The manager removed his hand. But, changing gears, he let his hand slide up her leg again. The secretary once again said, "Sir, remember rule 10 of our organization?" The manager apologized "Sorry miss but the flesh is weak." Arriving at the office, the secretary went on her way. On his arrival at the office, the manager rushed to look up rule 10 of the organization. It said, "Go ahead and be creative, failing should not stop you, continuous efforts may yield positive results."

Moral of the story: *If you are not well informed in your job, you might miss a great opportunity.*

Why my road to Success is always 'Under Construction'.

8

TEAM (TOGETHER EVERYONE ACHIEVES MORE)

(The Magic of Team Synergy)

Team - where work gets divided and success gets multiplied

Team (Together Everyone Achieves More)

If anything goes bad, then I did it.
If anything goes good, then we did it.
If anything goes very good, then you (Team) did it.

Before understanding teams, teamwork and team building, it is important for us to understand groups first.

What is a Group?

Two or more individuals, interacting and interdependent, who have come together to achieve particular objectives is known as a group.

The Journey of the Groups

• Inception

The first stage of journey of the groups is inception. It can be 'Structured' or 'Casual', some people come together on their own or they are brought together by someone with a structured plan to achieve pre-determined targets, members start interacting with each other, they seek and pass information, work together, depend on each other to achieve their goals together as a group to begin with.

• Impression

After formation, the most interesting stage is this 'Impression'. The group members start throwing their impressions on each other. This is a very natural process and this happens with all individuals.

Let me ask you, when you meet somebody, do you throw impression on others – Yes or No. Some of you will accept the fact and will say yes though some may say no, please note whenever we meet someone (know or unknown), we throw impression on others, believe me willingly or unwillingly this happens in all cases. The types of clothes you wear, colours you chose to wear is your impression you are throwing on others, where a person wearing red is giving impression of being confident the person wearing white can throw the impression of being cool, your hairstyle, your accessories, ornaments, watch, glasses, spectacles and footwear are your impression, your fashion, your blonde hair, ear pins, piercing, tattoos is your impression and we all do it expressively or inadvertently but we all do it regularly. Now you can raise a doubt that someone not wearing many colours and only putting up a sober look, no jewellery, no ornaments, no tattoos or anything is not throwing any impression on others. No he or she is also throwing the impression of being 'sober' on others, a saint wearing white or saffron is also throwing an impression of being different from the rest of the world, they also keep long hair and do not shave. This is also their impression to show the world that they are different from rest of the world, this is a very natural process.

If normal impressions are thrown on others, it is considered 'OK' but if extraordinary impressions are thrown, it can spoil the relationships and output in the group. Just imagine in a group of senior executives wearing business suites, if someone with blonde hair, hanging earrings, lip piercing, mutilated jeans, multicoloured T-Shirt and obnoxious footwear enters, how they will react? Do you think they will like to communicate with such a person who is not at all looking like a business executive and not in a business attire or a necktie.

- **Pathing**

After the shaking stage of 'Impressions' the next stage is Pathing where the path for all the group members is set, defined and finalised. After understanding each other's impressions, it is comparatively easy to distribute tasks as per their abilities, likings and inclinations, the duties are defined, the guidelines are given and the results are expected as per the impression created by the individual.

- **Action**

The result oriented stage of group journey is action, where all the group members act as per the roles and tasks assigned to them to achieve the pre-determined targets, as they are interdependent, successful performance of one member depends on the successful completion of previous member's task. This is just like a chain where one link is connected to other.

- **Parting**

The final state of Group journey is parting, after finishing the task the individual part their ways and move on, if the work or task of the group is complete, all the group members part their ways together, this is known as complete parting or it can be partial parting, where few group members part their ways. Parting can be happy or painful experience depending on the cohesiveness, task accomplishment, achievements together and chances of meeting or working again. (remember your parting with your school or college classmates, was it a happy parting or a painful one.)

Now before discussing TEAMS, let us learn something from the following story on team building.

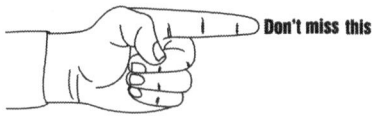

Hare and Tortoise

I am sure you must have heard the story of a hare and tortoise who had a competition and the tortoise beat the hare and we learnt the lesson that 'slow and steady wins the race'. I am sorry in my police career and now in the corporate culture, I have not seen this happening in this practical world. Steady people may win the race but surely not the slower ones.

I am going to share the story of modern (now corporate) hare and tortoise, which will be of your interest and learning, I am sure.

There was a hare and a tortoise working in an MNC. One day they had a heated discussion that who is better and they challenged each other for a race, the route and date were decided for the race.

On the day of the race a lot of people reached to witness it, some to praise, some to cheer up, some to pull the legs, some to laugh and some to just talk and walk (as you generally observe in any corporate gathering).

When the race started, the hare ran very fast and left the tortoise far behind, after sometime, he thought that tortoise can never beat him and he can win any time. He thought of taking some rest before finishing the race, he sat under the tree to relax and fell asleep.

The steady tortoise kept on running (rather walking) with the same gait and could surpass the sleeping hare and won the race.

The moral of the story is 'Slow and Steady Wins the Race'.

This type of story we all have listened in our childhood, but the modern corporate story does not end here. The hare, after losing the race felt bad obviously but did some soul searching also and realised that he lost because of overconfidence and carelessness. He thought if he improves on these weaknesses, he can win the race, so he challenged the tortoise once again and won the race with miles difference.

Now moral of the story

The fast and consistent will always beat the slow and steady.

If you have two people in your organization, one slow, methodical and reliable, and the other fast and still reliable at what he does. The fast and reliable will consistently climb the organisational ladder faster than the slow, methodical chap.

So it is good to be slow and steady, but it's better to be fast and reliable.

But the Hare story doesn't end here...

Team (Together Everyone Achieves More)

This time the tortoise did some thinking and realised that there is no way he can beat the hare in the race the way it was currently formatted. He thought for a while and challenged the hare for another race. This time the route of the race was different.

The race started and as a consistent and fast performer, hare took off and ran at the top speed until he came to a broad river, the finishing line was a couple of kilometers on the other side of the river.

The hare sat there wondering what to do now, as he could not swim so he could not reach the goal, in the meanwhile the tortoise reached (although slowly) to river bank, got into the river, swam to the opposite side of the river, crossed the river and continued running (rather walking) and won the race once again.

Now the moral of the story :

First identify your core competencies and then change the playing field to suit your core competencies.

In an organisation, if you are a good speaker, make sure you create opportunities to give presentations that enable the senior management to notice you. If your strength is analysis, make sure you do some sort of research, make a report and send it upstairs.

Working to your strengths will not only get you noticed, but will also create opportunities for growth and advancement.

The story still hasn't ended here...

The hare and tortoise, by this time, had become pretty good friends and they did some thinking together. Both realized that the last race could have been run much better.

So they decided to do the last race again, but to run as a 'Team' this time.

They stated off and this time the hare carried the tortoise till the riverbank on his back and then tortoise took over and swam across the river with the hare on his back. On the opposite bank, the hare again carried the tortoise and they reached the finishing line together quite early. They both felt a greater sense of satisfaction than they'd felt earlier.

They both were champions and they won the race in less time also.

Now, the moral of the story...

It's good to be individually brilliant and to have strong core competencies; but unless you're able to work in a team and harness each other's core competencies. You'll always perform below par because there will always be situations at which you'll do poorly and someone else does well.

Teamwork is mainly about flexible or situational leadership, letting the person, with the relevant core competency for a situation take leadership.

Note that neither the hare nor the tortoise gave up after failures. The hare decided to work harder and put in more efforts after his failure. The tortoise changed his strategy because he was already working as hard as he could.

In life, when faced with failure, sometimes it is appropriate to work harder and put in more efforts. Sometimes it is appropriate to change strategy and try something different and sometimes it is appropriate to do both.

The hare and the tortoise also learnt another vital lesson. When we stop competing against a rival and instead start competing against the situation, we perform far better.

Team (Together Everyone Achieves More)

Some teachings from this story

- Never give up when faced with failure
- Fast and consistent will always beat slow and steady
- Work to your competencies
- Compete against the situation, not against a rival.
- Pooling resources and working as a team will always beat individual outcomes
  Let us form and build stronger teams

There are many activities which only TEAMs can perform well and not Groups

Very obvious questions are - what are the teams? What is the difference between teams and groups? Are teams better than groups? Can we convert a group into a team? Can we achieve our goals more effectively in teams rather than groups. Let us start getting all answers one by one after understanding about teams first :

{ *Alone I am One, Together we are Ton* }

TEAM
(Together Everyone Achieves More)

A group in which the individuals have a common aim, the jobs and skills of each member fit in with others possessing complementary skills, is known as a team.

Difference between Groups and Teams

A group is a collection of individuals whose members share information and support each others to make decisions to help each other **'within'** his/her area of responsibility.

(Please note that group members are interdependent on each other and wait for one to perform first to proceed further on his / her output 'within' their areas of responsibility.)

Whereas in teams, apart from the requirements of the group, **collective efforts** result in the performance that is greater than the sum of those individual inputs which is known as **positive synergy**.

That means a team has got a magic - *'collective effort'* which produces *positive synergy*.

Collective efforts mean the push of all team members and the combined efforts. Just imagine people trying to push a static bus one by one, do you think the bus will move even an inch? No because all of them are just individuals and there is no collective effort. Now imagine these people joining hands together and doing a collective effort. They can move the static bus, they need not to put even that much of energy in pushing the bus, what they were putting as individuals.

The **positive synergy** can be defined as a combined output of a team, which is much more than the summation of individual efforts of the individuals.

We can here say that synergy means 2 + 2 = 5 or we can say 1+1=11, it may look mathematically wrong but this is a magical truth in management. Let me give you an example here by asking you a question – if you are preparing for your exams, how many chapters you can finish sitting all alone – your answer may differ but for the sake of understanding I will take the figure – 10.

Now how do you think your classmate / friend can finish, I again presume they are as smart as you are so again the figure is 10.

Now imagine you are good in one subject and (s)he is good in other, if you help each other you can finish about 25 chapters of two subjects. Here the outcome of individual performance was 10 + 10 = 20 and collective outcome is 25 from where this 5 additional output came, the answer is from Positive Synergy.

Team (Together Everyone Achieves More)

Apart from the teams the positive synergy also comes from different situations, to explain this point in detail, here is a small incident :

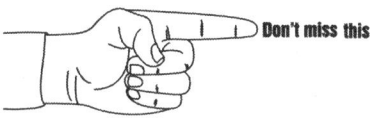

The Time Factor

A man was rushing towards the railway station as he was getting late, in place of taking a long way he thought of crossing a field from midway and asked the farmer in the field for his permission and inquired how much time it will take him to cross his field to the railway station.

The farmer answered it takes 15 minutes generally but if my dog spots you... only 5 minutes.

This is known as situational synergy.

Let us see another example of team synergy.

Just imagine you are sitting with your friend and preparing for the exam, check from your friend how much weight (s)he can lift, the answer may be 45 to 50 Kgs. Let us take the upper limit 50 Kgs, considering that you are also that much strong. Let us presume you can also lift 50 Kgs, now combined you both can pick up 50 + 50 = 100 Kgs.

Just imagine that someone, weighing 125 kgs in your family has got unconscious suddenly and you both need to pick him/her up and rush towards your car to take him/her to the nearest hospital. Don't you think you two will be able to do that, the answer is yes, it is possible and you will be able to pick up someone in trouble even if his/her weight is over 125 kgs, how this magic can happen, where you 'thought' that you can pick up 100 kgs combined and you picked up 125 kgs, again the credit goes to synergy.

What do we get most of the times - Groups or Teams

Now many years in corporate world from a junior level manager to Head of Department, I have found that most of the times you get groups, you need to convert them into teams, you will be lucky if you get a ready made team, which can be a dream come true but your abilities of converting a group into a team will decide your future in the organisation, your successful understanding of individuals and team building activities will play a magical role in your success, now the question is how to covert a group in a team :

How to Convert a Group into a Team?

First of all you need to believe that it is possible and you can convert a group into a team. What you need to do first is to make a rapport with all the group members individually and collectively. It will be a good idea to talk to them separately initially to understand them (as most people do not open up in front of others and do not want to share their feelings openly). Once you understand them separately, take them as a team for some sort of outing in an informal manner. It can be a lunch or tea party outside your working environment. From here onwards you need to take the following steps in converting groups into a team :

1) Give them a goal

Talk to them, understand their feelings and communicate, ask them what they want to achieve, discuss about their strengths, help in their areas of improvements and let them have a goal for themselves. If a group decided a goal for themselves, they will be putting the foundation stone to become a team.

2) Communicate like crazy

Never forget that communication is the key to success, communicate like crazy, the effective communication will solve all initial hiccups and you will be on the path of success in getting your dream team. If the members of the group are able to communicate freely among themselves they will find many friends and helping hands to be successful not only in their area of expertise but will contribute in overall success of the group (now becoming a team).

3) Problem solving should become a way of life

Swami Vivekananda has said that if you have not faced any problems and challenges in a day, you are not going on the right path.

You need to expect many obstacles in the path of converting your group into a team and should expect many problems and challenges to be solved and faced as a way of life and not as a part time activity. For teams the problems should come as a routine work, you understand them, discuss, solve and proceed further. If there is something you can't solve at present, don't worry, proceed further to see some more options and some more ways to solve it. If something can never be solved, why to take tension and why to bother, still proceed further, when the problems observe that you are not bothered by their interference, they will stop coming to you, and happy go lucky formula is 100 % successful in such cases. I am sure you must have heard that fortune favours the brave. This will bring quick responses and sharp reflexes in the team members and will pave the path of smooth transition of becoming a team from a group.

4) Make them Future Focussed

The group should be future focussed, they need to see beyond the horizon for a better future and then only they will invest in present and will forget the past. The future can be made bright only by forgetting about the past and working hard in present. Long-term planning should replace short-term objectives. They need to imagine how they will feel once they are successful and this will give them zeal to work harder for a bright, secure and rewarding future.

How much are you future focussed ?

While taking MBA classes, I have faced this question a number of times and have observed that many working executives and managers sacrifice their present for a brighter future, many of them ask me if this is right, few of them asked me the guaranty that if they sacrifice their present they 'will' be rewarded in future, what could have been my reply, can you try to answer this first.

As per my experiences of life, starting as a police officer and later embracing the corporate world, I faced this question many a times when I was sacrificing my present for future. I had a family to support and had many stakes to sacrifice. Can you ask your family to forgive you for the present so that you can invest all your time and energy for future which is neither certain nor sure. What could have been the best solution?

'Ati Sarvartra Verjayet' (excess of everything is bad) was my answer, yes it is true that without sacrificing your present you can't be successful in future but 'how much to sacrifice' is a question for which you need to find the answer yourself.

Over ambition has killed many and will not spare you if you try to cross the threshold limit. This is true for both individuals and companies, becoming future focussed is good but becoming 'extremely future focussed' or 'future focussed for a very long duration' is fatal. In place of making you, it will be breaking you, let us understand it with two examples from an individual and company's prospective.

Individual prospective of being extremely future focussed

Just imagine someone (imagining it on 'you' can be extremely painful) working hard to make a secure future, he/ she sacrifice a lot and invest time and efforts for a bright future, the person was and executive and now with hard work have reached to Managerial cadre, now what next, from a junior manager to a middle level manage and from a middle level manager to a senior level manger, becoming a Director, Vice President, General Manager and keep on thinking, working hard and keep on sacrificing many things for COO or CEO chair fast may kill his normal life charms, the physical and mental health can be at risk and even if he/she gets in senior cadre very fast sacrificing family, health or friends, what actually he/she will gain, to whom the person is going to show his new car or new office, who will come to him to share and celebrate his success as he is still future focused and have no time to talk to anybody, no time to show new car or office and now he is looking to become MD or CEO, there is no end to it. (More details are covered in the chapter of Spiritual Management)

Company's Prospective of being Extremely Future Focussed :

Imagine a company is very much future focused and expects its employees to sacrifice a lot for its future, no bonus is given as the money will be invested for future projects, no picnics are arranged, no games, no sports, no welfare activities as the money will be further invested... what will happen if employee are supposed to work hard, over time or for extra hours because a project is coming up, one project finishes, other one starts, one investment is done, now time for the next investment, company will need again everyone to work some more and this will become a never ending story, the employees will feel frustrated and will leave such organisations, the organisation will be surprised and shocked how employees are leaving such a growing organisation and they will call professionals like us to ask what went wrong and we will say 'Ati Sarvartra Verjayet'.

5) *Support Creativity*

You will find in a group the members looking towards their manager for further instruction when you start converting it in a Team. More creativity and creative talents in the group will help you convert that group into team as they will be coming up with amazing solutions and new ways and means to tackle the challenges in better manner, this will not only help the team in facing difficult challenges but will also increase Teamwork.

To explain this point let me share a very interesting story from Japan which will clarify the importance of supporting creativity and how the company got benefited with it :

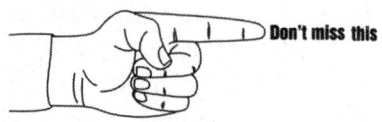 Don't miss this

The Soap Box Story

There was a soap manufacturing company in Japan and they got few complaints from their customers that they have got empty soap boxes in the cartons they bought, the company felt very sorry, investigated the matter and came to know that this happened because of a fault in automatic packing system, what they observed was that there were two conveyers at soap packing station, the soaps were coming on one conveyer and empty boxes on the other, the machines was inserting the soaps in the empty boxes and it got sealed in cartons, what they observed is that on first conveyer if the soaps are not coming machine was not able to put the soap in the box resulting packing the empty box only, which become the reason of complaints.

The board meeting was called and suggestions were asked to solve this problem, someone suggested a laser sensing machine to be connected with the machines to recognise if the boxes are empty while packing, but it was very costly, some suggested the X - ray machine for that but again this idea got rejected because of heavy cost and they could not reach any conclusion which was effective, full proof and cost effective.

If you are a Leader (or Manager) of that department, how will you solve this problem?

Playing the role of a true leader, the manager of the department discussed this with his team and expected some creative ideas to solve this problem, some people must have criticised that why something like this should be discussed with workers and what they can suggest

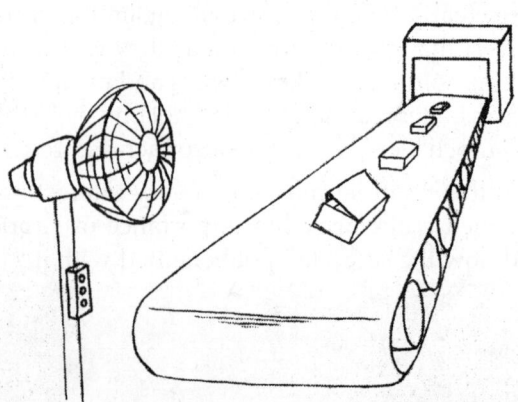

for such process related matters, but the departmental manager was knowing the values of individual contributions and creativity.

A worker gave a very practical and cost effective solution of this problem, he advised the management to put a pedestal fan near the conveyer and if the box is empty it will fly off as it is light weight without a soap in it, before getting packed into cartons.

The manager was pleasantly surprised and rewarded the worker for his creative thinking and for such a practical and cost effective idea.

6) *Make Them Understand the Magic of Positive Synergy and Common Aim*

Once the group understand the magic of Positive Synergy they will work collectively for a common aim (there is huge difference between 'One Aim' and 'Common Aim')

If there is one aim for all individuals and if some of them leave that aim, it is not going to impact others and if one aim is 'shared' by Team Members, it becomes - 'Common Aim', if it is achieved, it helps everyone in the Team.

Let me ask you a question to clarify if you have understood the difference between One Aim and Common Aim.

Example :

A bus is going from Connaught Place to Gurgaon and all the people travelling have bought ticket from CP to Gurgaon, they all have got same aim to go to Gurgaon, now what is this, it is a Group or a Team, is there 'one aim' or 'common aim'.

Try to answer before you read further for answer :

If half of the people decide to de-board the bus mid-way at Dhaula Kuan, what will happen to rest half of the people, do you think they will be bothered even for rest others, the answer is no, that is why this is only 'one aim' and not the 'common aim' as this is a group, yes if there is a Cricket Team of students going to Gurgaon to play a cricket match over there and half of the team members decide to de-board mid-way then of course the other half cannot play match in Gurgaon and now this is a shared aim known as Common Aim as the impact of decision is on all the Team Members.

7) Let Members Enjoy complementing each other's Work.

The motto of any Team is :

The Show Must Go On...

And one of the biggest magic is the 'Complementary Skills', the team members complement each other with their abilities and works because they want to ensure a continuous show, somebody is present or not is not going to stop their progress and they complement each other's works, because their Moto is - the Show Must Go On...

Example :

A few days back only, the whole India cheered as Indian Cricket Team lifted the World Cup, if you observe the performance of all players, they complemented each other quite well, wherever required, for an example in the Semi Final match against Pakistan, when Batsmen could not do very well and got out around 260, bowlers complemented the batsmen and bowled out the Pakistani Batsmen only within 230s.

Now in Final Match, it was the turn of Batsmen to complement Bowlers, when the Sri Lankan Team scored 270s and bowlers could not contain them under 250s the Batsmen complemented and scored more than that to win the Final Match and lifted the Cricket World Cup.

Complementary skills are not only shown in one's own area of expertise but it can be in someone's area also, for an example you must have seen Indian Batsmen like Sachin, Sehwag and Yuvaraj Singh balling to complement bawlers and Bowlers like Harbhajan Singh and Zaheer Khan scoring many runs to complement Batsmen.

Team Building

Team building applies when you are building a team in the first place or amalgamating two teams to form a new entity, or completely reconstituting and revitalising an old team.

What to see in Team Members while Building Teams

A. Ability to Perform as Team Members

Some people may be great individual contributors, they can achieve big results related to them only when they perform individually but when we go ahead in making Teams, first quality we need in team members is to check the ability to perform as team members. Even if some individuals can perform good individually they fail miserably when they are expected to perform in Teams, as the one who can work with others should have quality to help and support others, listen to others, sacrifice his / her own view points for the sake of the team and ready to give credit to someone else for his/her performance.

Generally if you observe people who play games like Chess, Swimming, Tennis or Badminton (singles) etc. are individual performers and people playing Cricket, Football and Volleyballs type of Team Games are Team Players.

B. Helping Attitude

The ability of the individual to perform in all circumstances is not enough as a team member, another important quality what leaders look for is the Helping attitude, team members who help others get helped in their efforts, which became the foundation stone of their success as Teams.

C. Subject Knowledge

Another important aspect is of course the Subject Knowledge, upto the time it is clear with the Leader that the individual has got a strong subject knowledge, the leader will not take him to his team as without that neither the team member will be able to help other members nor he will be able to contribute in the success of the Team.

To understand the concept of Great Team Building, let us read a short story of a Team of two Thieves who were very successful in their endeavours.

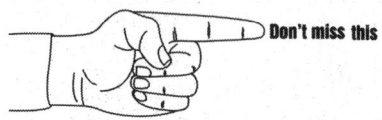

Story of Two Successful Thieves

There was a gang of two thieves. They were very successful as they could climb across many big walls, could enter high rise buildings and run away with valuables. One day someone asked the secret of their success and one of them said that the secret of their success is team work, when they are obstructed by a big wall one offers his shoulders to others to step up and climb the wall. The other one also after climbing does not forget the one who offered his shoulders and offer his hand to pull the first thief to the wall.

What we learn from this story is that if we offer our shoulders to our team members to climb up, do we offer them first? Do we have confidence and patience that when they reach on top they will pull us? Does the person who has climbed the ladder of success by placing his feet on somebody's shoulder forget the one who helped? Does he pull the person also up when he establishes himself up there and do both of them help each other in crossing the challenges.

Biases in Teams – How to Deal with Favouritism

The way cancer is considered to be the biggest disease in human beings, biases are considered to be the biggest disease in team building. May it be natural but biases can harm the spirit of team building. The following is the list of some biases which creep up in teams with possible solutions to tackle with such biases.

Favoritism

Leaders sometimes favour some employees. They recruit only those who are known to them so favoritism is quite common. If subordinates are from same region or share common language, favoritism happens but leaders should keep one thing is mind that taking favours will never help them in achieving long term goals and they should not be very much worried about short-term objectives. Now what is the solution to this challenge -

The Solution -Equidistant Approach

The best solution to avoid favoritism is to keep equidistant approach by the leader or manager. He or she should keep him/herself equally away (and equally close too) to all the team members, to be successful in equidistant approach, the following points should be kept in mind:

- **Never Speak in Regional Languages**

If you are a Punjabi, you would love to speak in Punjabi with a Sikh gentleman in your team, and if you are from Bengal, you would like to listen the sweet language from your Bangla speaking colleagues but always avoid this in a team, speaking in regional language is considered favouring people from your region. It is considered as bad manners as other team members are not able to understand your communication and you will be accused of favouring colleagues from your region.

Always speak in the language the majority of your team understands or the acceptable language like Hindi or English, of course if you are in a particular region such as Kerala, speaking Malayalam will be absolutely fine.

- **Keep the Performance Appraisal Process Open and Crystal Clear**

Those who are not promoted can accuse you of favouring those who got promoted so keep the performance appraisal process open and clear to all team members, everyone should know the achievements of all team members. Those who deserved, if promoted or given good increments will feel happy and motivated, even others also will appreciate and respect the system, it will not only motivate all team members but will help you in putting the strong foundation of 'justice for all' system in place.

- **Praise in Public - Reprimand in Private**

If your conduct is like an open book there cannot be any accusation of any sort of favouritism. You should praise in public (which you should do thrice a day with different team members), letting everyone know that you have observed the sincere efforts and you can motivate publically. If at all you need to Reprimand, do it in Private, so that others are not horrified and disheartened, the person who is Reprimanded in private also respects the system as your aim is to correct the system and not to insult the person in front of others, even if there is a personality problem, it can be improved with guidance and counselling.

Discipline in Teams

Should there be discipline in teams? What do you think?

Teams can be successful only with (positive) discipline, who will do what, with whom, who will support when and how all the tasks are divided as per the inclination, taste and ability to perform will define the basic guidelines of discipline.

Imposed Discipline or Self Discipline

Gone are the days of imposed discipline when somebody was standing on your head to check if you have done whatever is expected from you. If you are working or not and if you have done something which is prohibited and if you were found guilty, you were punished publically, remember those days when you were asked to stand on the bench for not doing your homework.

This is the age of self discipline (and positive discipline) which helps us in achieving un- scaled heights of success, where responsible leaders and subordinates decided what to do, how to do and how soon to finish a task with guiding principles. I always ask what is the use of pointing fingers on those who are sometimes 'late' but contributing the most for your business, why can't we be liberal to the level of human acceptance so that their contribution can be seen and not the so called 'punctuality'.

Issues in Teams and How to Deal with Them

• Mistrust

This is a common phenomenon, the team members start trusting the leader and other members slowly and gradually only when they feel and see them trustworthy and helpful. You need to help many a times voluntarily to take (rather expect) the respect.

• Work Load and Work Distribution

Can you distribute the workload equally among the team members – think for a while as a leader and answer. The right answer is - No, it is not practically possible just like you can't divide a cake equally for everyone, someone will get a cherry and someone a bit more cream but none can be satisfied with equal share. Everyone will feel the other person has got the bigger pie, here in the team everyone will feel that they are overburdened and others are not having any work matching their workload, which may be just an impression, but this can create some problems. The best solution to this issue is the Role Clarity, if the roles are clear there are few chances of tussle between the team players.

The Donkeys and Monkeys in the Teams

The work is divided keeping in view the donkeys and monkeys in the team. The donkeys (those team members) are quiet and hard-workers, they will not say anything if you give them more work, they may grin a bit but will eventually accept additional workload, they are born to do more work and they are hard workers. The monkeys on the other side are those members who have never worked, never want to work and never let others work, they will keep on jumping from one table to another and from one office to another for gossip, grapevine and for collecting and giving information which they call real communication for organisational effectiveness. If you need to divide the workload, give finance type of laborious works to donkeys and sales type of supporting works to monkeys (see how easily you can guess whether you are a donkey or monkey).

- **Leadership Biases and Leadership Abilities**

Knowingly and unknowingly, leaders become bias, when I was doing a personal research on the 'Personal Biases' and the impact of 'Impression Management', a lot of managers acknowledged that they are biased, they asked me why should not they be biased in the favour of the team members who are sincere, hard working and never say no for any work given to them, they told me that they are negatively biased towards the work shirkers, malingers and who have somehow managed to get the appointment even if they were not on merit. Leaders confess that they show they are not biased but create positive situations for those they trust and believe. Even it happened with me, I also felt it loud and clear when my British boss supported me left, right and centre and made sure that I go to for a foreign trip for a training programme and ensured that I take my family to spend some more days and enjoy my life, of course he was biased towards me - positively biased as he knew that I am going to make sure that I teach and train many team members after my foreign trip. Of course it happened and I trained in return about 600 employees in a short span of time.

The unbiased behaviour and equidistant approach majorly depends on the leadership abilities to handle, perform and negotiate in different situations, you do not get the dream team anyway although the efforts should be to convert the existing group or team into a dream team. Sometimes I have asked myself a question, how many times, I will have to endeavour to convert existing teams into dream teams and the answer came from a spider and its web – upto the time I want to survive, I need to keep on converting it.

- **Interpersonal Conflicts**

People come from different backgrounds and with different attitudes that is why it is quite natural to have interpersonal conflicts. It is not only the duty of the leader to make sure that these are solved and taken care of correctly but also it is his moral responsibility to make sure that the team members understand that these are because of different prospective and each team member should respect the views of others so that they work together, respect each other and achieve 'common goals'.

- **Effective and Constructive Feedback**

Giving effective and constructive feedback to team members is an art and I learnt it from some of my superb trainers of an International University in one of their management development programmes. I am sure you will buy my view that there will be all types of team members in our teams (or in organisation), some will be good, some not so good, some will be smart, some may not be, some will be intelligent, some not that aware and some will be helping and some always seeking help. When they will perform their duties, they will do something good or bad, now the important duty of the leader is to give them effective and constructive feedback so that they come to know where they are doing good, where not so, where they are performing, where they are not able to, where they lacked, where they did not, what they could achieve, what they couldn't. Generally I felt that first time leaders sweat in giving effective and constructive feedback, either they are too soft that the team members did not take them seriously or they are too strong that team members may get horrified, after a poor feedback the performance of team members may drastically go down. Now how to give feedback is an interesting lesson to learn not only for first time leaders but for those who were not very successful in giving effective or constructive feedback in the past. Let us see what is the 'Burger' rule of giving effective and constructive feedback.

'Burger' Rule of Giving Effective and Constructive Feedback

What is a burger? Soft and cushiony from top, soft and cushiony from bottom and hot (and valuable) in the middle.

Same should be the style of constructive feedback, when you start, start with positive feedback, praise the team members for what they have done good and positive, make a rapport of a positive and effective leader, then come on the main (hot) and important points, use firm but soft language, discuss everything in plain language with clear words. Say something you think team members can take negatively by prefixing – 'I think' this is like this, if you feel that team member is understanding and accepting it, convert 'think' into 'believe' and if the impact is negative and team members are not accepting it, clarify that you were just 'thinking' for further homework.

Never attack on anybody's personality and always talk about the reasons of shortcomings, as we generally say **'Hate Crime and Not Criminal'**. Instead of explaining everything sometimes asking questions is a good idea and let the team member (or mentee) reach on the conclusion him/herself. Sometimes what is not acceptable is loud and clear to the subordinate but what is acceptable is not clear, explain and tell them about the expected behaviour.

For an example : if you are counselling someone not to smoke cigarettes in office then you need to explain where is the smoking zone to smoke.

Now in Burger Style, the closing of feedback session should also be very cushiony and soft, you should close the session with a positive back pat and positive remarks, mentioning some positive points about the team member's (mentee) personality.

So like Burger, the feedback should be soft and cushiony from top (in the beginning) and bottom (at the end) and hot and important (valuable) from inside.

Management Lesson
The Beggar

A beggar found a Rs. 100 note and decided to have a great dinner in a 5 star hotel, he enjoyed the dinner and when the bill of Rs. 2000 came he said I have got no money, the hotel manager called the police and handed over the beggar to him.
The beggar gave Rs. 100 note to policeman and got free.
This is called management.

Success is a relative term, it brings so many relatives.

9

MOTIVATION FOR A NEW 'YOU'

(First for Self then for Others)

Need is the seed of Motivation

I want to start this most important chapter with an awesome story on motivation of a painter.

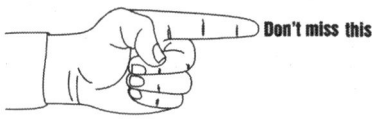

The Masterpiece

There was a very passionate painter. Many of his paintings got huge appreciation but he was not satisfied with his own work. He wanted to make a masterpiece that no one had made in the world. And therefore he started working on it and after many days of hard work made an awesome painting. He was very happy and excited to show it to others, this being his masterpiece.

He showed it to his teacher first and he was very happy and felt honoured to be his mentor. His teacher advised him to place it on the main crossing of the city so that people could see this. The painting was hanged on the main crossing and almost everyone saw it. Some praised it and some criticized it, after finding some faults in it.

The painter was disheartened to see people pointing fingers and finding faults in his masterpiece and got sad. His teacher observed this and told the painter not to lose his heart as people have got the habit of finding faults and criticising almost everything.

Teacher advised the painter to place a clean board with some brushes, colours and whatever is required for someone to paint with a message besides the masterpiece:

Please paint this masterpiece again on the clean board removing the fault you have noticed.

Guess what happened, no one could paint such a marvelous painting on the clean board, as it was easy for people to find the faults but painting without any fault was not possible for anyone.

The painter got the confirmation that it is not a weakness in his art but a weakness with people to criticise anything and everything they see.

(I am sure some people will criticise my masterpiece (my book) also but I will request them to please come up with their masterpiece without any mistakes and with everything I have missed in this book.)

A winner is not one who never fails, but one who NEVER QUITS!

Defining motivation will attract words like encouraging, inspiring and guiding but I will quote one of the most suitable definitions of motivation given by the Ex-Chairman of Institute of Management Technology – Prof. (Col.) P. S. Bajaj, who is my mentor, as per him :

Motivation is the process of activating a dynamic and dormant force in a person, which once activated, makes him/her perform better and better.

Motivation is the willingness to exert high levels of efforts towards designated goals conditioned by the effort ability to satisfy some individual need. It is a force that activates dormant energies and sets in motion the action of the people. It is the function that kindles a burning passion for action among the human beings.

Let us motivate ourselves from some of the most motivational stories from all over the world, which teach us the value of motivation. If despite big problems they could succeed, we also surely can. For those who are committed to success have no excuse of failure and their luck also favours them. Let us see these motivation stories first :

In 1936, **Jesse Owens** arrived in Berlin (Germany) to compete for the United States. Adolf Hitler was using the games to show the world a resurgent 'Nazi Germany'. He and other government officials had high hopes that German athletes would dominate the games with victories (the German athletes achieved a "top of the table" medal haul with 89 medals - 33 Gold, 26 Silver and 30 bronze). Meanwhile, Nazi propaganda promoted concepts of "Aryan racial superiority" and depicted ethnic Africans as inferior. Owens surprised many by winning four gold medals on August 3, 1936 in the 100 m and 200 m sprint, long jump and 4 x 100 m relay.

In 1954, not long after, a boy failed an audition for a local vocal quartet - the Song fellows. He explained to his father, "They told me I couldn't sing." In April, he began working for the Crown Electric company as a truck driver. His friend Ronnie Smith, after playing a few local gigs with him, suggested he contact Eddie Bond, leader of Smith's professional band, which had an opening for a vocalist. Bond rejected him after a tryout, advising him to stick to truck driving "because you're never going to make it as a singer." **Elvis Pressley** became of the most popular and successful singer in the history of America.

> *Self-Motivation is the key to success, it opens the door of growth and it locks the bad luck.*

Wilma Rudolph was the 20th of 22 children. She was born prematurely (4.5 lbs) and her survival was doubtful. When she was 4 years old, she contracted double pneumonia and scarlet fever, which left her with an infantile paralyzed left leg. At the age of 9, she removed the metal leg brace she had been dependent on and began to walk without it. By 13 she had developed a rhythmic walk which doctors said was a miracle. The same year she decided to become a runner. For the next few years every race she entered, she came in last. Everyone told her to quit, but she kept on running. One day she actually won a race, and then another; from then on she won every race she entered. Eventually this motivated girl, who was told she would never walk again, went on to win 3 Gold medals in 1960 Rome Olympics.

In 1962, four nervous young musicians played their first record audition for the executives of the Decca recording company. The executives were not impressed. While turning down this group of musicians, one executive said, "We don't like their sound. Groups of guitars are on the way out." The group was called the **Beatles** and later won 7 Grammy awards.

Flying Sikh - Milkha Singh has been an Indian athlete and considered to be one of the greatest athletes the nation has ever produced. He was born in 1935 at Lyallpur (now in Pakistan) and had a very difficult childhood when he saw his parents and relatives being killed in front of his eyes during the Indo-Pak partition massacre. A 12 year old Milkha escaped for his life hiding himself behind the corpses in the train to India and managed to get a lease of life though left all alone in this world. He has been the only Indian till date to have broken the Olympics Record, still he lost the bronze medal in the 400m event at Rome Olympics Games 1960 by just 0.1 second.

Milkha Singh tried to get into the Army 3 times, but was rejected. Finally, his brother Malkhan Singh helped him get into the electrical and mechanical engineering branch of the Army in 1952, and it was there that he participated at the first sports meet of his life. Later he won Gold Medals in both 200m and 400m events at the Tokyo Asian Games 1958, at the Cardiff Commonwealth Games held the same year, he grabbed a gold medal again. In Rome Olympic Games 1960, Milkha, who was initially leading the race, finished just 0.1 second and lost a bronze, he defeated the Fastest Pakistani runner Abdul Khaliq who had won a 100m gold medal at Tokyo Asian Games 1958, in the year 1962, and the Pak President Ayub Khan named him 'The Flying Sikh', a name that has became immortal forever in the history of Indian Athletics.

> *"If I find 10,000 ways something won't work, I haven't failed. I am not discouraged, because every wrong attempt discarded is another step forward.*
>
> ***Thomas Alva Edison***

These were a few stories of motivation and I am sure you must have felt motivated and energetic and must have thought that if they can do that, why can't I or if this can happen to them why not to me, etc.

The Need is the Seed of Motivation

What is Need?

Needs are deficiencies and are created whenever there is a physiological or psychological imbalance.

Have you observed that someone who is just back from work, so tired that he doesn't want to move from sofa or bed for any household activity may jump with joy and start playing, leaving all his tiredness aside with a child or may happily go for a movie with friends or will be ready to play even outdoor games with friends. This is fulfilling a 'need' of the person.

Types of Motivation

Motivation is mainly of following 4 types; you just have to see which one is more applicable for you in which situation. After understanding the following types, you will agree that different types of motivation is suitable for different type of people, read the following types to know the most suitable type of motivation for you : -

- **Positive or Incentive Motivation**

If someone promises you a reward or award to do something, it will be known as a positive or incentive motivation, where you get positive results or you get incentive for your deeds.

- **Negative or Fear motivation**

It starts with a negative feeling or fear which drives you towards achievement of some goal or aim, threatening someone that he / she will fail if they do not study or they will lose their job if they do not achieve their targets. This is a motivation where fear works.

- **External Motivation**

This motivation comes from outside world and flows inwards to make someone inspired to work hard; eventually it has to become an internal motivation in the long run to be effective.

- **Internal Motivation**

It starts from within the individual, people who are self-motivated always motivate others irrespective of the fact that they are their juniors, seniors, friends, relatives, colleagues or anybody.

> *A motivated person is one who can lay a firm foundation with the bricks others have thrown at him.*

Positive or negative motivations can be Internal and External or a combination of both.

Why to wait for *Jamwant* (who inspired and motivated Hanuman by reminding him about his powers) in our life, can we be self-motivated, is it possible to learn the basic lessons of self-motivation is the question I am going to answer here. The people who are self-motivated succeed easily and do not need any external push to perform well.

Let us see some of the characteristics of self motivated people.

- They are always good in time management.
- They believe and practise positive and effective communication.
- They are of cheerful nature and have a good sense of humour
- Their subject knowledge is unmatched and they keep on learning new things.
- They are flexible and can adjust themselves as per the need of the hour.
- They are having learning and adaptable attitude and keep on learning new skills which may help them in succeeding and never stop learning from anyone who knows more than them.
- Humbleness and politeness are the inseparable qualities of their personality.

- They are good human beings, honest and sincere to their work.
- Self esteem is very precious to them and they live with very high self esteem.
- They recognise other's needs and keep on guiding and inspiring others.
- They are always emotionally balanced.
- They know how to manage stress because it is not possible to avoid it all the times.

Tips to Increase Motivation

'What' and 'How' are two questions you need to get answers in life. 'What' may be known to most of the people but they do not know 'How' which can be the turning point. Most of my MBA Students ask me 'How' to increase the Motivation and I always give them some tips, which are essentially required to increase your motivation level. The following are some of such tips, which will surely help you in increasing your motivation.

- Set your (SMART) goals (SMART means – Specific, Measurable, Achievable, Realistic and Time bound Goals)
- Exercise leadership qualities you have learnt or acquire new leadership qualities from those who are successful and practical.
- Understand other people psychologically and try to be in their shoes.
- Start establishing a two-way and open communication.
- Start respecting all people around you, irrespective of your relations and status.
- Start establishing an enability climate in your society/ organisation.
- Show interest and concern for people and keep them challenged and excited.

- Make each team member an integral part of your dream team.
- Encourage your team-members to do their best and then support their efforts.
- Avoid being biased for / against any team member.
- Make efforts to exercise good human relations at work showing concern for the team members.
- Treat team-members fairly with respect and consideration.
- Train and develop people to attain relevant skills and knowledge.

Socrates, Aristotle, Alexander, Adolph Hitler, Napoleon Bonaparte, OSHO Rajneesh, Stalin, Sir Winston Churchill, Mahatma Gandhi, Lenin, Netaji Subhash Chandra Bose, Rani Laxmi Bai, Mata Jija Bai (Mother of the Great Warrior and King Shivaji), Chanakya and Chandragupt Maurya were some of the personalities who knew all the tricks and traits of motivation. They all motivated the people around them in such a way that even today the world remembers them for their motivational leadership styles.

People like Dr. APJ Abdul Kalam, Swami Ramdev, Asim Premji, Anna Hazare and NR Narainmurthy are alchemists (in Hindu mythology 'paras' can turn any metal into gold with its Midas touch) they not only have proved themselves but can turn others also very positive and motivated.

> *Motivation is very contagious, it spreads fast with positive people, grip the negative ones also and make them seriously successful.*

Motivation is directly linked with performance, if you perform well, you feel more motivated and remember – motivation is a process (and not an activity), so you need to keep on taking actions continuously up to the time you get favourable results.

Motivation for a New 'You'

Generally positive thinkers are motivated, one of the best ways of increasing self-motivation is to start thinking positive, but first you need to know if you are a positive thinker or not, do you want to know this, give a small test down below :

Are you a Positive Thinker

This is a simple test, you just need to read the following situations and tick the feelings which will come in your mind in such a situation.

Situation:

Just Imagine that one of your family member (consider your father or mother if you are not married and your wife or husband if you are married) has not returned home today and it is quite late, generally that family members is back by 7 pm but today it is 10 pm but there is no phone and no information, you called on his / her mobile but there is no response, you called his / her office and came to know that he / she has left at 6 pm only, you called at many places where he / she can go like a friend's place or to relatives but there is no information, now you are tense, very tense as there is no communication. Now the question is what type of the following feelings will come to your mind, tick the feelings which you have in such situations :

1. He/she must have met with an accident; we may get a call from some hospital.
2. There must be some problem, he/ she must have hit somebody on road and police must have arrested him/ her, soon there will be a phone from police station.
3. He/ she must have been busy in office and due to the burden of work must have forgotten to call at home.
4. Somebody must have kidnapped him / her and soon there will be a phone call for ransom.
5. He / she must have won a lottery and have gone to collect a huge sum of money, in this happiness, have forgotten to inform at home.

6. He / she is very annoyed with some family dispute and that is why have decided to stay with some relative / friend today and have not informed us to put us under pressure or to teach us a lesson.
7. He/she must have lost mobile and have gone to purchase a new one that is why he/she is late.
8. He / she have decided to commit suicide because of family problems and economic conditions and have committed suicide somewhere by now.
9. This is a hit and run case, he/she must be lying in a pool of blood on some road.
10. Must be enjoying some office party and may not be able to know the phone ringing and that is why not picking up the phone.

Task:

Tick the feeling which will come in your mind if one of your family member has not returned today up to 10 pm without any information.

Result:

If you have ticked up point numbers : 1,2, 4,8 or 9, write 'N' against your answers.

If you have ticked up point numbers : 3,5, 6,7 or 10 write 'P' against your answers.

Count total 'N's and total 'P's and is if your Ns (Negatives) are more your thought process is negative and if your Ps (Positives) are more, your thought process is positive.

If your thought process is positive, well done, congratulations, you are on the right track, keep it up but if your thought process is negative, do not lose heart as you are with majority of people who cannot think positive without proper training and streamlining the thought process in a positive manner.

Remember the first step of training is always being careful if your thoughts are positive or negative and second is to throw out the negativity from your mind and replace it with positive thinking. Gandhi's formula of being ready for the worst will surely help you out, life is life, you cannot mould outside situations always, you can just work on yourself, start doing that, for further details on increasing the motivation, read the following useful points.

Ways of Increasing Motivation (for Individuals)

1. Clarify Your Ultimate Goal

Running without a goal may demotivate anyone, having a goal in front and continuously knowing how much path have you covered to attain that will surely motivate you. This clarity of mind will give you enough strength to achieve it at any cost and this zeal will keep on increasing your motivation, you just need to make sure that you keep on working and moving ahead towards your goal.

2. Do Not Try to Prove Anything to Anyone

You need not to prove anything to anyone, your sincere efforts are for you and make sure that you work to achieve your goals in place of impressing others, rather you need to impress yourself with hard work and sincerely beyond your limits and this will surprise you pleasantly.

3. Practise Sense of Humour

People those who are serious type with grumpy faces are not able to mingle up with others, if you want to be successful, you need to mingle up with people of all walks of life and the best adhesive is the sense of humour. People around you will be looking to spend time with you if your sense of humour is good, this will also keep you on lighter mood for best results. One thing you need to keep in mind is that you need to accept people as they are, do not try to change them instantly, the law of nature is that they will change observing your personality on their own.

4. Be Ethical

In all circumstances be ethical to take the side of honesty and truthfulness. With false feelings you may achieve false success, the long-term true success is found on the ethical path only, we call it long-term success. Never be hazed with short-term achievements although short-term actions should lay the foundation stones of your long term success, respect your situation and condition to accept whatever has happened to you in true sense, blaming God or others will not help you at all, accepting the defeat and knowing the reasons to work upon the challenge will help you in succeeding for sure.

5. Believe in Yourself

Believing in your abilities has been discussed in the chapter on abilities in this book; you need to thank God for the brain, body and blessings of life you have got. If you determine you can bring the change, you surely can. Not only the belief in your abilities only but the abilities of your team also helps you out in achieving your goals.

6. Balanced Approach

True success can be achieved with a proper balance between planning and execution, further strengthening your abilities and improving on your weaknesses will give you a long-term prospective of success. No one can be successful in a day and the plan has to be chalked down properly keeping the abilities and weakness in view, you should invest some time for physical and mental health (many people do not know anything about mental health, one should understand that being successful you need to be both physically and mentally fit. Eat healthy food, exercise, read and listen to motivational material to be balanced and successful.

> *The difference between a loser and a winner is that loser plans but winner executes also.*

Ways of Increasing Motivation (for Organisations)

1. Implement Strict Work – Life Balance

The first mantra to improve the motivation level of your organization is to implement strict work – life balance. In this age of competitive world where people are otherwise putting their heart and soul to survive in the cut throat competition and putting a lot of time in travelling on overcrowded roads or being pressed in public transports, we need to take care of them, as this has reduced their family time drastically. Most of them look (actually they are) intelligent but they are tense from inside because of the increasing imbalances of professional and personal life which are creating undue pressures. Maintaining quality of work and at the same time having a happy family life will make your organization a quality organization to work for where people in other companies will be willing to join.

I have worked in great places and have converted a company as one of the India's top 100 companies to work for. Let me share one secret - we gave a lot of attention to quality of work and personal life and we got amazing results. Offering flexible hours can solve many issues, employees feel motivated as they can take care of their personal challenges and this reduces the turnover ratio and increases loyalty scores drastically.

2. Employee Relations Activities

We all need some entertainment, not necessarily at home but at work also, employees should be given opportunities to mingle up in informal gatherings also. This not only increases togetherness but brings the team spirit also. Picnics, Cultural Programmes, outdoor learning and development programmes, quiz competitions, sports & games competitions, Birthday Celebrations and Award & Reward programmes are considered to be the best in employee relations activities. This will lead your organisation towards becoming a great place to work.

3. Training and Development Programmes

The growth of the company is directly proportionate to learning and development activities in that company. You keep on conducting such programmes and keep on making your employees knowledgeable, skillful and intelligent and they will keep on contributing with more vigour and dedication towards the growth of the company. Remember the relationship of employees with company is like wheels and car. You keep on rolling wheels ahead, the car will keep on proceeding further.

4. Recognising Employees

Generally in the race to win, employees keep on contributing sometimes going beyond the call of their duty. Awarding and rewarding them is an integral part of recognition. If due to some reasons you are not able to spend money on rewards or awards, simple back-pats, saying thank you publically, giving appreciation letters and acknowledging their hard work are other ways of giving them due recognition. This not only motivate employees, who have contributed but those also who are thinking of contributing or have the ability to contribute.

5. Participative Management

One very interesting formula to motivate your employees is to implement participative management, which means taking participation in decision making activities from employees, encouraging them to join work councils, making them board representatives, challenging them to come up with quality circles. I am sure they will amaze you with unexpected high results as they start feeling that it is their work, their challenge and their decision. They love their contribution and love to see the company growing because of their participation, some companies even invite their employees to take ESOPs (Employee Stock Ownership Plans). When the employees see that the company's growth is dependent on their contribution, they contribute to their level best and when they see that they are also having a share in the company's profits, they even strive harder to make companies into revenue generating systems. We have seen sometimes putting a variable pay linked to output (in cases of sales or production output) has given amazing results.

6. Career and Succession Planning

Which employee will grow, how they will grow, what will be their career path if they stay in company, whom they can succeed on what position, what are the qualifications and competencies required for them to grow and how they can achieve these competencies, who can help them in learning skills and competencies required to be on higher levels in organisational hierarchy are the questions if answered properly and supported, employees see a bright and promising career in the company. Their first aim will be towards company's growth as the company grows, they will grow automatically.

7. Culture of Respect and Honour

The most important aspect in increasing motivation in a company is to change its culture towards respect and honour, employees should be expected and trained to respect each other across levels. There should be one cafeteria, one library and one recreation room for all levels of employees. Gone are the days when the facilities for manager were separate or different foods were served on managerial levels. We should believe in equity and should give respect to all employees, all works and all departments across organisation.

On the lighter side, enjoy the following management lesson.

Management Lesson
The Boss

When the body was first made, all the parts wanted to be boss.

The brain said, "I should be boss because I control the whole body's responses and functions."

The feet said, "We should be the Boss as we carry the brain about and get him to where he wants to go." The hands said, "We should be Boss because we do all the work and earn all the money."

And so it went on and on with the heart, the lungs and the eyes until finally the ass hole spoke up.

All the parts laughed at the idea of the ass hole being the boss. So the ass hole went on strike, blocked itself up and refused to work.

Within a short time the eyes became crossed, the hands clenched, the feet twitched, the heart and lungs began to panic and the brain fevered.

Eventually they all decided that ass hole should be the boss, so the motion was passed.

All the other parts did all the work while the boss just sat and passed out the shit!

Lesson:

You don't need brains to be a boss - any ass hole will do.

If there is a day between two dark nights, then why the hell there is one sunday in Seven working days.

10

THE SPIRITUAL SPIRIT

(The Ultimate Goal)

Never say – Oh God, how big is my problem, rather say – Oh problem, how big is my God.

You must be surprised how spiritual management will help you in becoming a successful manager or a human being in life. I know and have seen a lot of managers who make good money but are not happy in life. In this chapter, we will discuss some interesting concepts of life, which are required to be learnt and understood completely to be 'Happily Successful' in life. (This is not about IQ or EQ, this is about SQ — Spiritual Quotient)

Concept 1 : Value of Money

Let us understand this concept with the help of an interesting story of Keshav and his farmer father – Vikrant.

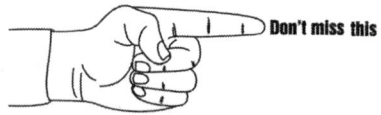 Don't miss this

Value of Money

There was a farmer – Vikrant, who used to worry a lot for his son Keshav who was very extravagant. He would spent his whole pocket money on his friends in a day only. Vikrant wanted to teach Keshav a positive lesson to learn the value of money.

One day when Keshav was going out to play, Vikrant told him to get Rs.10 while coming back.

Keshav got sad and sat outside his home thinking how to earn Rs. 10. His friends came and asked him the reason of his sadness, Keshav explained the whole story and one of his friends asked him to relax

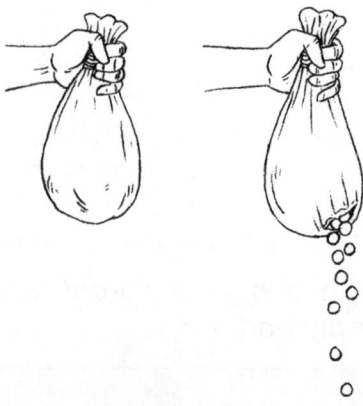

and take the money from him. Keshav took the money and they all left happily to play.

That day Keshav returned back with Rs. 10 given by one of his friends and handed over it to Vikrant. Vikrant took the money and threw it in the well. Keshav saw this but said nothing, he thought his job was to get money. What Vikrant was doing with the money was none of his business.

Next day the same thing happened, again Vikrant expected Keshav to bring Rs. 10 back home and again he sat quietly outside his house. Again his another friend offered him Rs. 10 and took him away to play. Keshav came back that day also with Rs. 10 and again Vikrant threw the money in the well. Again Keshav thought the same that how he is bothered, Vikrant is throwing the money into the well or putting in the fire, was none of his business.

The days kept on passing, every day, one or the other friend was giving money to Keshav who was handing it over to Vikrant to be eventually thrown in the well. A day came when all the friends of Keshav stopped giving any more money to him. Rather they stopped playing with him as it was a costly affair on everyday basis.

One day no one came for Keshav's rescue and he had to approach Kathuria, another farmer for some work. Kathuria gave him a lot of work to do for the day. Keshav started the work and was quite tired in few hours only. He was digging, making cues to water the field, his clothes got dirty and he started perspiring profusely. He started huffing and puffing badly. By lunch time he was totally exhausted as he had never worked that much in his life and was on the verge of collapsing.

He sat down for a while as his hands were full of boils and he was in a lot of pain. He approached Kathuria to get the money for the half work done.

Kathuria was annoyed as Keshav left the work in between and could not complete so gave him Rs. 5 only. Holding Rs. 5 in his hand tightly, Keshav rushed towards his home and handed over Rs. 5 to Vikrant and as soon as Vikrant was about to throw Rs. 5 into the well, Keshav stopped Vikrant and held his hand to request him not to do so as it was his 'first earning', which he had earned with great difficulty. Vikrant understood the feeling of his son and embraced him tightly as now he understood the value of money - the earned money.

I think this lesson should be taught to all spendthrift children, if they know how difficult it is to earn they will spend accordingly and will not waste money at all.

Concept 2: In Comparison to What...

Have you noticed that we generally complain about a lot of things on daily basis. We have got issues about our salaries, benefits, perks, cars and mobiles and what not? Why for most of us the salaries are less, cars are small, houses are not fully air-conditioned and mobiles are not the classy BlackBerries. Let us put a yardstick against each one of these and start asking ourselves – "In comparison to What"?

We have got houses big or small but there are some who don't even have a hutment. We have got two wheelers to ride or cars to drive and some are not even able to walk without help. We get salaries every month because we are employed, whereas some are pushed in crime because there is no job. Some people are ailing with diseases with no cure and some are spending the remaining days of their life in old age homes.

We are morally answerable to them as they are also the part and parcel of our society and we should help them out accepting our social responsibility. The following story of two friends will help you out in understanding this concept in further detail.

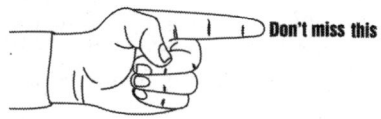

The Story of Two Friends

Let me share a very interesting story with you all...
What you have to do is to note all the bold words in the story and then we will do an exercise after you have finished reading the story till end.
One day two very old friends Ram and Shyam met after many years and felt very good. They met after about 20 years and now both of them were around 40 years old. They shared with each other everything about their family, job and challenges.
Ram said that he was **very happy and successful** because he was **healthy** and working with a bank as a manager and takes a **handsome salary** of Rs. 50,000/month. He **spends time with his happy family** of three, his wife and 12 year young daughter,

The Spiritual Spirit

studying in 6th class. They all go for **outings, swimming, etc** in his **Maruti 800** and was very happy to lead a **happy family life**.

Shyam said that he was **not very happy and not that successful** in his career in **comparison** to his teammates as he is **just a** vice president in an MNC and **only makes** about 2,00,000/month. Has **a Skoda** but is always **very busy** and have **got no time for family**, his son is **probably in 5th or 6th class** and is **suffering with many modern diseases like hyper tension, blood pressure and heart problem**.

Both of them were confused and surprised.

Ram thought, How lucky Shyam was. He is very successful as he is a VP only at 40, owns a big car, makes very good money, what else does he need in his life.

Shyam thought, How lucky Ram was. He lives a healthy life, spends quality time with his family and enjoys life, has got everything in his life that is required to be happy.

Now a small exercise for you :

1. Note down all the Bold words in the above story, read what Ram thought about Shyam and what Shyam thought about Ram. Analyse who is right and why?

> *Rat race is rat race, even if you win, you will remain a rat only*

2. Ram said he is successful in life, is he right?
3. Shyam said he is not that successful in life, is he right?
4. What will you advise Ram and Shyam to remain happy in life.
5. Success is what – money, health, family life, happiness or achievements?

If given an option what would you like to become - Ram or Shyam.

What is the aim of your Life?

Think for a while before answering...

I am sure it is not very easy for many people to answer this question as they have never ever thought of any such aim of their Life, for them life is life and they need to live it somehow, they work very hard to live this life, sacrifice a lot, study a lot, work a lot and want to gain a lot. What they want to gain is most of the time quite materialistic (like house, car, jewellery etc.). What they want to achieve is to lead a **comfortable life,** and to make it comfortable they do a lot of uncomfortable activities. They want to make a lot of money so that they can buy big happiness in life like plush houses, big cars, roam around the world and can eat best of the foods.

Some of them work very hard to earn all these and they inculcate a habit of tension. They keep on working hard and feel tense for years and it becomes a habit, rather a very strong habit. Even if they achieve what they aspire, they do not stop working and worrying hard as they have acquired a habit in past many years. They need to pay heavy opportunity cost for their standard of living. Sometimes it can be even their health, family life and relationships or friends. They do not think if it is worthwhile to make the money on the cost of the family or health.

A very strange fact of life about mankind is :

They spend first half of their life in making money losing their health, and spend second half of their life in spending that money in regaining lost health.

What if you lose your health and family life and lead your life in pain, is that you worked very hard for? Did you make a lot of money so that you can give it to the posh hospitals or you wanted to give all the happiness of life to your **kids.** I have heard many people saying that they are doing all this for their children, so that they can live their life comfortably.

Are you sure your children will be thankful to you for making a lot of money for them even if you were not there on their birthdays, sports days or parents teachers meetings because you were so busy in making money, gaining success and proving others that you are smarter than them.

I know some questions of priority of job or family are difficult to answer and some will argue that if they do not work they will not be able to support their families that are perfectly OK if you think otherwise. The following amazing story will give you some insight to learn how to remain happy in life.

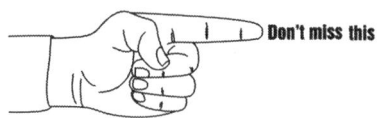
Don't miss this

Story of Aamir and Slave
Once upon a time there was a very rich Aamir (Sheikh) in Arab. He was blessed with a lot of wealth - jems & jewellery, bigger houses than palaces, cattles, servants, slaves and many more things which a common man can only dream. He dealt in oil and owned many oil wells but he was not happy. He always wanted to be more rich, more influential and more respected.

One day he travelled towards Africa for some business and came across a very healthy and energetic slave (this is a story of the time when slavery was common on earth). He liked the slave and bought him at a high cost.

The slave travelled from Africa to Arab without knowing his fate but trusting in God and with the belief that 'it's all for the best'. When Aamir reached his house he called his wife and proudly showed the slave boasting his bargaining skills. Aamir's wife was happy and praised his choice and innocently asked the name of the slave, as Aamir also did not know, he asked his wife to ask it from the slave directly.

When Aamir's wife asked the name from the slave, she got an amazing statement. He said- "what's in a name, what can be the name of a 'Slave', there are no choices with slaves, you can keep whatever name you want to, whenever you call me with that, I will run towards you for your help."

Aamir and his wife were highly impressed with his answer and started thinking, how true he is. He is not even choosing a name for himself. Is 'choicelessness' a pain or bliss in life? While they were thinking, they realised that the choicelessness shown by the slave was very soothing and in the first day only they started liking him.

Aamir's wife was happy with the healthy slave and wanted him to remain healthy. She asked the slave about his food habits so that they can offer him the appropriate food.

> It is not the failure but the fear of failure, which prevents us to take any action in life.

She got another amazing statement from the slave again, he said "food choices for 'slaves', there is no choice of food for me, whatever God has determined for me, I will get that, why to complain and why to expect, I will accept anything given by you as a reward from God and will eat it happily".

Aamir and his wife were already impressed with the positive attitude of slave and his theory of choicelessness of life. They started thinking about the understanding of life's important principles by the slave.

Continuing the conversation, Aamir told the slave that they wear cardigans in Arab but African's wear different clothes, what will be his choice, so that he can feel comfortable?

The slave again smiled and said – "I will thank my God for the matter that I am alive to wear something, I will be happy in anything decided by you because you are my 'masters' now, how can I expect my 'master' to act as per 'my' wishes, I need to mould myself as per my master's choices and I will happily accept anything decided by you, if I do that, I can never be sad."

Aamir got a shock of his life, the positive attitude of slave highly impressed him and he started thinking that probably this is the reason why the salve is very happy with life and he is not. A big question came to his mind, that if he is the 'master' of the slave and slave is very happy with whatever he is deciding, then for Aamir, the 'God' is the master, whatever the God is deciding should be acceptable to Aamir, may be because he is demanding more from his 'master' (God) is the reason of his sorrows and unhappiness.

Today he learnt a lesson, probably the most valuable lesson of his life to enjoy 'choicelessness' in life. He understood that he will remain happy if he accepts happily whatever is given by God, of course he should strive for more, work hard to get it and achieve it with his abilities but has to learn to remain happy in all circumstances.

Concept 3 : Managing Stress

What is Stress :

A dynamic condition in which an individual is confronted with an opportunity, constraint or demand related to what he/she desires and for which the outcome is perceived to be both uncertain and important.

Two types of Stresses: Positive and Negative Stress

Positive stress pushes you positively to achieve something and you run against the time lines. Some people claim that they can concentrate in studies only when the exams are on their head.

The negative stress is what which destroys you mentally and physically. The continuous stress leads you to high or low blood pressure, headaches, uneven pulse rates, heart diseases, anxiety and depression.

Can we learn how to avoid stress

The expected stress can be avoided up to a very limited extent, for an example if you know that you will be stressed in examination days because of huge course material, you can start reading from day one to avoid this stress in future. But if you ask me about unexpected stress (which is 90% of the times) - I will say no, we cannot learn to 'avoid' such stress, stress is like a wind, it can come from any side - up, down, left or right, if it has to come, it will come, you can only learn how to 'manage' it rather than 'avoiding' it. For example if you come to know you have been selected for a reality TV show, you will surely be stressed (positively of course).

Learning how to manage the stress is the best way to cope up with it.

The following can be the distressing activities as per individual taste and inclination :

- Yoga and Meditation
- Aerobics / Running or Going to Gym

- Dance
- Sports & Games
- Music
- Playing / Spending time with Kids or Quality time with Family
- Spending time in the lap of nature
- Hobbies (like photography, gardening, etc.)
- Outings / Recreation facilities
- Joining Spiritual sermons / religious places, etc.

Sometimes people put so much stress on their mind for very little achievements. The following story of 'One Bedroom Flat' will justify the fact that sometimes the 'opportunity cost' is too high for some achievements.

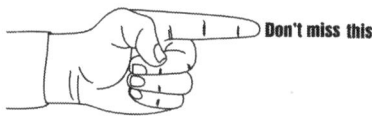
Don't miss this

ONE BEDROOM FLAT...
WRITTEN BY AN INDIAN ENGINEER...

A Bitter Reality

As the dream of most parents I had acquired a degree in engineering and joined a company based in USA, the land of braves and opportunity. When I arrived in the USA, it was as if a dream had come true.

In place of Asking the God – why me, ask the God – 'Try Me'.

Here at last I was in the place where I wanted to be. I decided I would be staying in this country for about 5 years in which time I would have earned enough money to settle down in India.

My father was a government employee and after his retirement, the only asset he could acquire was a decent one bedroom flat.

I wanted to do something more than him. I started feeling homesick and lonely as the time passed. I used to call home and speak to my parents every week using cheap international phone cards. Two years passed, two years of burgers at McDonald's, pizzas, discos and watching the foreign exchange rate getting happy whenever the rupee value went down.

Finally I decided to get married and told my parents that I have only 10 days of holidays and everything must be done within these 10 days. I got my ticket booked in the cheapest flight, was jubilant and actually enjoying hopping for gifts for all my friends back home. If I miss anyone then there will be talks. After reaching home I spent one week at home going through all the photographs of girls and as the time was getting shorter I was forced to select one candidate.

I thought I would have to get married in 2-3 days, as I will not get anymore holidays. After the marriage, it was time to return to USA. After giving some money to my parents and telling the neighbours to look after them, we returned to USA.

> Human beings live as if they will never die and die as if they never lived.

My wife enjoyed this country for about two months and then she started feeling lonely. The frequency of calling India increased to twice in a week sometimes 3 times a week. Our savings started diminishing.

After two more years we started to have kids. Two lovely kids, a boy and a girl, were gifted to us by the almighty. Every time I spoke to my parents, they asked me to come to India so that they can see their grandchildren.

Every year I decided to go to India... But part work part monetary conditions prevented it. Years went by and visiting India was a distant dream. Then suddenly one day I got a message that my parents were seriously sick. I tried but I couldn't get any holidays and thus could not go to India ... The next message I got was that my parents had passed away and as there was no one to do the last rites the society members had done whatever they could. I was depressed. My parents had passed away without seeing their grandchildren.

After couple more years passed away, much to my children's dislike and my wife's joy we returned to India to settle down. I started to look for a suitable property, but to my dismay my savings were short and the property prices had gone up during all these years. I had to return to the USA...

My wife refused to come back with me and my children refused to stay in India... My two children and I returned to USA after promising my wife I would be back for good after two years.

Time passed by, my daughter decided to get married to an American and my son was happy living in USA... I decided that I had enough and should wind up everything and returned to India... I had just enough money to buy a decent 2 bedroom flat in a well-developed locality.

Now I am 60 years old and the only time I go out of the flat is for the routine visit to the nearby temple. My faithful wife has also left me and gone to the holy abode.

Sometimes I wonder was it worth all this?

My father, even after staying in India, had a house to his name and I too have the same nothing more. I lost my parents and children for just ONE EXTRA BEDROOM.

Looking out from the window I see a lot of children dancing. This damned cable TV has spoiled our new generation and these children are losing their values and culture because of it. I get occasional cards from my children asking if I am all right. Well at least they remember me.

Now perhaps after I die it will be the neighbours again who will be performing my last rights. God Bless them. But the question still remains 'was all this worth it?'

I am still searching for an answer.................!!!

START THINKING, IS IT JUST FOR ONE EXTRA BEDROOM???

LIFE IS BEYOND THIS .....DON'T JUST LEAVE YOUR LIFE .... START LIVING IT ....

Concept 4 : Good Professional - Good Human Being

For last many years, working in HR, I get to read many resumes, meet many people in interviews, seminars and workshops, some of them are very smart, some very gentle, some have got good professional knowledge and some are just good human beings but not that good professionals. Some are good professionals but bad human beings, what we should be and what we should pick – good human beings or good professionals, to understand this concept, the following matrix will help you out, my ex boss – Subir Vyas with whom I worked in Gap, helped me out in understanding this concept.

The Professional - Human Being Matrix

	Low	High
High (Humanity)	IV Bad Professional Good Human Being	III Good Professional Good Human Being
Low (Humanity)	I Bad Professional Bad Human Being	II Good Professional Bad Human Being

Professionalism

In above matrix you will find professionalism on X axis and humanity on Y axis, let us move quadrant wise to understand this concept.

Quadrant I : Of course no one would like to have or to work with a person who is not a good professional and not a good human being, but sometimes we find this category of people in some organisations we work. They are there because of their luck, some of them somehow entered by virtue of their known people on higher positions in those companies and some of them were just blessed with such jobs where neither they could become good human beings not they could learn the tricks and trades of the business they are in. They just keep on passing time sometimes even disturbing others and not letting them work. They play politics and get taste in harming others, they get sadistic pleasures in their deeds and my advice is to just remain away from them but whenever you come in their contact. Your behaviour should be good as they generally do not harm the people who behave nicely with them even if their 'damage potential' is very high. They generally form sycophant societies where they do crib sessions, blame others and company for their failure and spoil others. (concept dedicated to my ex boss – Wg. Cdr. S. L. Soni, The Oberoi, New Delhi).

> *Never Say – Oh God, How big is my problem, always say – Oh Problem, how Big is my God.*

Quadrant II : Very interesting quadrant, without reading further, first you decide if you would like to work with these type of people who are good in their work but are bad human beings, they can do the best of the work but they backbite and harm others. Their skills and abilities are good but they play politics, of course your answer is going to be - No, however I will say that these type of people can be chosen (if there is no alternative left) for the jobs where you need only individuals to perform the job and they are not supposed to deal with other people. Otherwise also we do not need a driver, carpenter or electrician to be a very good human being in all cases, if they are good in their work, we can manage with them.

Quadrant III : The best combination of people is this quadrant, they are good human beings and good professionals too. This is the combination which is considered to be the best, these people are self motivated and know their job well, we can call them self motivated people as they love their work, accept challenges and are self driven people, but there is only one problem, this is a very rare species. They are hardly found and are not left by their bosses. You should be in this quadrant by all means, if you need to improve on your skills, start working immediately and if you think you need to improve yourself for sure for this quadrant, you are reading the right book.

Quadrant IV : This is the second highest category in demand and the second best combination after Quadrant III. You can train on your skills if you get a good human being with positive attitude.

Hire on Attitude – Train on Skills

Hire on attitude and train on skills is my formula from years together. I have seen people those who are good human beings with positive outlook and who quickly pick up the skill level desired. It is generally said that training someone on some skills is easier than changing someone's attitude. If you do not get Quadrant III people for your teams, you can opt for Quadrant IV.

 **If you keep on buying things you don't need, pretty soon you will be selling the things you need.**

Concept 5 : Character

Before understanding the concept of character, let us know what happened with Ram Sir first...

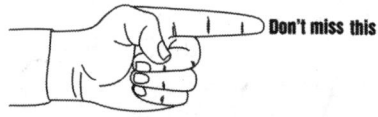

What is Pure Milk ?

Ram Sir was a very famous and successful yoga teacher and health consultant. One day one of his friend and pupil told him that just as the sun rays are for the whole world and not only for a particular region, knowledge of Ram Sir is also for the world. He also predicted that soon the fame of Ram Sir will spread throughout the world and he will have to go to other countries to teach Yoga.

And as predicted by his pupil cum friend, Ram Sir was invited to Germany to teach yoga to Germans and he stayed in a 5 star hotel in the place known as 'Bhramastra' near Berlin.

The steward asked if there is any special breakfast request for Ram Sir for the next morning. Ram Sir said that he will be thankful if a glass of 'pure milk' is send to his room for breakfast, the steward noted down the request but he could not understand the order – 'pure milk' ?

The Spiritual Spirit

Now the confused Steward reported the matter to his restaurant manager and told him that he understands the term milk but what is 'pure milk', he has never heard it. The restaurant manager was also confused and he approached his food and beverage manager along with the steward and informed him about an order for room service breakfast - pure milk.

The food and beverages manager who was quite experienced in beverages also got confused as he also could not understand 'pure milk'. They thought of checking it with Ram Sir himself and approached him and asked about 'pure milk'.

Ram Sir explained them that pure milk is milk in which no water is added.

The food and beverage manager of the hotel said – 'Sir, that is milk, why should one add water in that to spoil it and if it is milk, why are you calling it 'Pure Milk'.

The Germans could not understand why somebody would mix water in milk, if their guest is paying for milk, he will get milk, of course without any water content.

Ram Sir understood that he comes from a place where you need to say 'pure milk' to get unadulterated milk and where people have strong character, you get only milk and not 'Pure Milk'.

The lesson we have learnt from the above incidence is that it is the characters of individuals which makes the character of the society and the combined character of society makes the character of the country.

Management Lesson
Anyway

People are often unreasonable, illogical and self-centered;
Forgive them anyway.
If you are kind, people may accuse you of selfish, ulterior motives;
Be kind anyway.

If you are successful, you will win some false friends and some true enemies;
Succeed anyway.
If you are honest and frank, people may cheat you;
Be honest and frank anyway.
What you spend years building, someone may destroy overnight;
Build anyway.
If you find serenity and happiness, others may be jealous;
Be happy anyway.
The good you do today, people will often forget tomorrow;
Do good anyway.
Give the world the best you have, and it may never be enough;
Give the world the best you've got anyway.
You see, in the final analysis, it is all between you and God;
It was never between you and them anyway.

A bus station is where a bus stops.
A train station is where a train stops.
Today I came to know why my desk is known as work station.